China's Ongoing Agricultural Reform

China's Ongoing Agricultural Reform

Colin A. Carter
Professor of Agricultural Economics,
University of California, Davis

Funing Zhong
Professor of Agricultural Economics,
Nanjing Agricultural University, Nanjing

Fang Cai
Deputy Director of the Population Research Institute,
Chinese Academy of Social Sciences, Beijing

Research sponsored by
The 1990 Institute

The 1990 Institute

Copyright © 1996 The 1990 Institute

All rights reserved

First published 1996

No part of this work covered by the copyright herein may be reproduced or used in any form or by any means without permission in writing from The 1990 Institute.

The 1990 Institute
651 Gateway Boulevard, Suite 880
South San Francisco, CA 94080

Printed in the United States of America

Library of Congress Card Number: 96–069840

ISBN: 0–472–10814–X

Contents

Foreword	vii
Acknowledgments	ix
List of tables	xi
List of abbreviations	xiii

1. Introduction 1
    Key Findings and Recommendations 6

2. Major Policy Developments in Agriculture 8
    Basic Features of the Reform 8
    Stages of Economic Reform 14
        The First Stage (1978–1984) 15
        The Second Stage (1984–1988) 16
        The Third Stage (1988–present) 18
    Other General Issues Associated with Agricultural Reform ... 20
        Environmental Effects 20
        Farm Size 21
        Property Rights and Land-Tenure Issues 23
        Domestic Regional Trade 24
        International Trade 26
    Summary 28

3. The Slowdown of Agricultural Output Growth 30
    Alternative Explanations for the Slowdown 31
    Analysis of County-Level Production 32
    What Led to the Productivity Slowdown? 35
    Summary 38

4.	**The Role of Markets**	**40**
	Reform of Product Markets	41
	Reform in the Input Markets	46
	Land	46
	Labor	46
	Other Inputs	47
	The 1993–1995 Food Price Increases	48
	Summary	51
5.	**Excess Labor in Agriculture**	**53**
	Rural Population and the Agricultural Labor Force	55
	Excess Labor and Out-Migration from Agriculture	60
	Policy Options for Addressing the Problem of Excess Labor	66
	Summary	68
6.	**Township and Village Enterprises**	**69**
	Total Factor Productivity Growth in TVEs and SOEs	73
	Explanations for the Success of TVEs	76
	The Impact of TVEs on Agricultural Production	77
	Summary	78
7.	**Rural Financial Flows**	**79**
	Income Transfers through Pricing	79
	Budget Transfers	82
	Induced Capital Outflows	84
	Farmers' Investment in Agriculture	87
	Summary	88
8.	**Conclusion**	**89**
References		**91**
Index		**99**

Foreword

The 1990 Institute is proud to present this important study on China's agricultural and rural reform by Professor Colin Carter, Professor Funing Zhong, and Professor Fang Cai.

This study is published at a time of heightened worldwide interest in the Chinese economy. Spectacular economic growth in China has spurred speculation that the nation will surpass Japan as the second largest economy in the world in the next century. Recent conflicts between China and the United States have sharpened the awareness of how little the world knows about the enormous changes that have taken place in China's economy in the pass seventeen years and of the implications of those changes for the rest of the world. This in-depth study makes a significant contribution toward filling the void.

Despite China's rapid industrialization, more than three-quarters of the 1.2 billion population live in rural areas, and 73 percent of the rural labor force are engaged in agriculture. Thus, agricultural reform affects the livelihood of the majority of the Chinese people. Moreover, rapid industrialization has widened the gap between urban and rural incomes, resulting in growing unrest in the countryside. Rural poverty and excess rural labor have emerged as the most pressing policy issues in China. In addition, policymakers must find ways to feed the growing population on constantly shrinking cultivable land.

These and other related issues are probed in depth and with sound scholarship by Professor Carter and his distinguished co-authors. Their findings will command the attention not only of policymakers in China but also all students of the Chinese economy and of economies in transition from socialism.

Foreword

The 1990 Institute was founded in 1990 in the United States by a group of individuals concerned about China and wishing to help the Chinese people without becoming involved in the politics of either country. They shared a conviction that the most effective way to improve the welfare of the people in China was through enhanced understanding of the social and economic barriers that have held back China's modernization. Although busy in their own professions, they freely contributed their time, talents, and money to establish this organization. With the support of individuals, corporations, and foundations, the Institute has been able to sponsor and publish major studies, and organize several international conferences on economic reform in China.

In late 1995, the president of the Institute was called upon to serve on an advisory committee to help the Joint Economic Committee (JEC) of the U.S. Congress organize a comprehensive study of China's economy and its implications for U.S. policy toward China. The Institute's scholars have been invited to contribute essays on various aspects of the Chinese economy, including an overview, for the volume scheduled for publication in 1996 under the auspices of JEC.

The Institute and all its volunteer associates are encouraged by this recognition. They invite those interested in China to join them in their continuing effort to support research on China, a country of rising importance in the world.

Hang-Sheng Cheng
President, The 1990 Institute

San Francisco
July 1996

Acknowledgments

We, the authors, are indebted to The 1990 Institute in San Francisco for providing resources to complete this book. In particular, we are grateful to Hang-Sheng Cheng, President of the Institute. Mr. Cheng approached us with the initial idea for this book and he provided encouragement and provocative questions throughout the writing process. Frederick Crook, D. Gale Johnson, and Scott Rozelle contributed insightful comments on an early draft, which helped to shape the final book. Bin Zhang was a research assistant on this project and we thank him for his backing.

We received valuable cooperation and support from several individuals and institutions: The University of California, Davis, Nanjing Agricultural University, and the Chinese Academy of Social Sciences provided institutional support. We would like to acknowledge individual assistance received from Professor An Xi-Ji at Beijing Agricultural University; Mr. Guo Shutian, Ministry of Agriculture in Beijing; Mr. Zhu Xigang, Chinese Academy of Agricultural Sciences; Professor Justin Lin and Professor Hai Wen, China Center for Economic Research at Peking University; and Mr. Du Ying, Research Centre for Rural Economy, Ministry of Agriculture, Beijing.

* * *

The Institute wishes to acknowledge a generous donation from Jonathan and Cynthia Wilcox that made possible the research for this study. Additional funding for research and the publication of this book was provided by the Sung-Kwok Foundation of San Francisco, a private foundation established by Beulah Kwok and C. B. Sung.

Acknowledgments

The Institute also wishes to thank the following: Addison Design of San Francisco for the initial book jacket design for this series; C. J. Huang for providing the Chinese calligraphy; Dae Advertising for assisting in the graphics for the jacket of this book; the University of Michigan Press for handling the worldwide distribution of the books published by The 1990 Institute; and Rhona Johnson for editorial and production services.

Tables

Table 1	Real Growth Rates (percent) of Gross Value of Agricultural Output, 1979–1993	12
Table 2	Grain Production in China, 1978–1994	13
Table 3	Regional Grain Production Efficiencies, 1978–1984 and 1985–1992 (percent)	33
Table 4	Government and State Enterprise Construction Investment, 1976–1992	38
Table 5	Free Markets in Urban and Rural Areas	42
Table 6	Grain Procurement by the State, 1978–1993	45
Table 7	International Comparison of Employment in Agriculture	56
Table 8	Farm Labor as a Share of Rural Population by Province	57
Table 9	Comparison of *National Population Census* and *Statistical Yearbook of China* Data on Rural Labor	59
Table 10	Rural Household Support Ratio, 1989–1992	59
Table 11	Estimated Rural Labor Demand by Province, 1990	62
Table 12	Estimated Rural Labor Surplus by Province, 1990	63
Table 13	Capital Intensity of TVEs, 1984–1993	64
Table 14	Employment Elasticities for TVEs, 1979–1993	65
Table 15	Gross Output Value of Total Society, Industry, and Agriculture	70
Table 16	TVEs: Major Economic Indicators	72
Table 17	Procurement and Free Market Prices for Rice and Wheat, 1985–1990	81

Table 18	Estimated Rural–Urban Income Transfers through Grain Procurement, 1985–1989	81
Table 19	Government Net Budget Transfers to Agriculture, 1979–1994	83
Table 20	Net Budget Transfers to Rural Areas, 1979–1994	84
Table 21	Rural Financial Transfers through Rural Credit Cooperatives, 1979–1993	85
Table 22	Agricultural Financial Transfers through Rural Credit Cooperatives, 1979–1993	86
Table 23	Individual Farmers' Investments in Agriculture, 1982–1992	87

Abbreviations

AYC	Agricultural Yearbook of China
FAO	United Nations Food and Agriculture Organization
FSU	former Soviet Union
GDP	gross domestic product
GNP	gross national product
GVAO	gross value of agricultural output
HHH	Huang-Huai-Hai (River Basin)
HRS	household responsibility system
MLY	Middle and Lower Yangtze (River Basin)
NCAR	National Committee for Agricultural Regionalization of China
NPK	nitrogen, phosphorus, potassium
RCC	Rural Credit Cooperative
RMB	Renminbi: China's currency, which is denominated in yuan
SOE	state-owned enterprise
SSB	State Statistical Bureau
TFP	total factor productivity
TVE	township- and village-owned enterprise
USDA	United States Department of Agriculture

CHAPTER 1

Introduction

The overall purpose of this book is to evaluate the success of the economic reform of China's agriculture and to discuss current issues concerning agriculture in China. Continued economic growth in the agricultural sector and integration of the rural–urban economies is critical to ensure China's transition away from being a lower-middle-income country. Although China's rural economy has grown rapidly since the 1978 reforms, there remains an important division between the rural and urban economies that will impact future growth.

In real terms, the overall economy is four times as large, and the agricultural sector two and one-half times as large, as it was in 1978.[1] China's agriculture has experienced a major economic transformation. As an illustration of the effects of overall reform on food markets, Figure 1 shows the rapid growth of per capita food consumption of three key food items (meat, fish, and vegetable oil) resulting from income growth. Over this period, both real per capita income and per capita meat consumption increased by more than two and one-half times.

Agriculture's share of national income has fallen from around 30 percent to 20 percent since 1978. The declining relative importance of agriculture is a normal trend for a developing country. For many years, China's agricultural sector has been taxed in order to support industrialization (Lardy 1983; Lin, Cai, Li 1994). This is not unusual: many countries with incomes comparable to

---

1 See Lardy (1994, pp. 14–18) for a discussion of the problems associated with measuring the size of China's economy in internationally comparable terms. Converting China's gross domestic product (GDP) from yuan to U.S. dollars, using the official exchange rate, yields a low figure of about $400 per capita. However, this underestimates the real purchasing power of incomes in China. Lardy reports that alternative estimates, using the purchasing power parity approach, range from $1,000 to $2,600 ($U.S.) per capita. He suggests that a "prudent" estimate (for 1990) is approximately $1,100 per capita, which is about three times the estimate based on the official exchange rate.

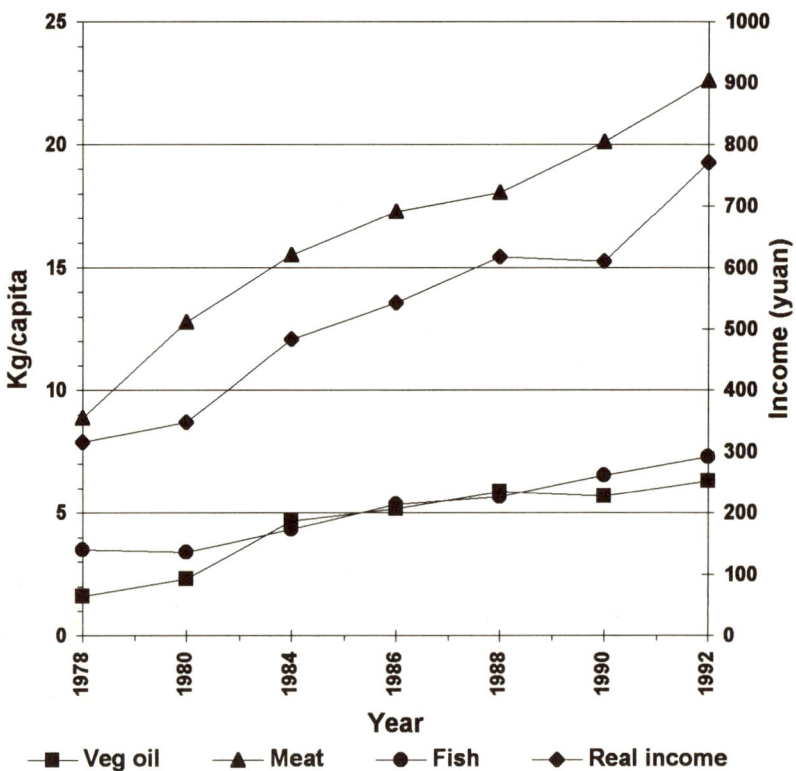

Figure 1. Income and per capita food consumption: 1978–1992. Note: Real per capita income is on the right-hand scale.
Source: Compiled from the Statistical Yearbook of China, *1994 (SSB, 1994).*

China's have followed a similar strategy up to the point at which agriculture becomes a small share of the economy (Anderson 1990). Beyond that point, the typical response of governments in other Asian countries has been to subsidize agriculture. It is doubtful, however, that China's agricultural policies will soon copy those of Japan, South Korea, or Taiwan by shifting from taxation to subsidization as China's per capita income increases. The situation in China is unique for the following reasons:

- Over 70 percent of the total population lives in rural areas, and thus it would be very difficult to subsidize the majority of the population.
- Most of the urban industrial sector (i.e., state enterprises) is owned by the government, and it is unlikely that the government would tax its own enterprises to support agriculture.

- The central government places large weight on the economic well-being of urban residents and thus emphasizes the importance of keeping food prices low.

Prior to economic reform, farm products were classified into three categories, according to how they were sold by farmers. The first category was *unified* procurement commodities, which included grain,[2] cotton, edible oil, and oil-bearing crops. The government was the sole buyer of these commodities through compulsory quotas and fixed prices. The second category, *dual-track* commodities, included meat and aquatic products, tobacco, tea, silk, and sugar. The government set compulsory procurement quotas and prices for these commodities, but permitted free-market sales for any surplus production above that necessary to fill the government quotas. Third, there were *zero-quota* commodities, consisting primarily of fruits and vegetables. Although there were no compulsory quotas for these commodities, the lack of market infrastructure meant the government had a dominant position in the procurement and marketing of these goods.

The growth of China's agricultural economy since 1978 has reflected the impact of agricultural policy reforms across all three categories of farm products. The major policy changes were: the privatization of farming through the household responsibility system (HRS); the support of rural industrial development (i.e., township and village-owned enterprises [TVEs]) to enhance the overall rural economy; and the reform of mandatory procurement quotas and prices for agricultural commodities. The first wave of liberalization came in the late 1970s and early 1980s with the dismantling of the commune system, the introduction of the HRS, reduced restrictions on open-market sales, and the encouragement of TVEs. The second wave came in the mid-1980s through liberalization of the unified procurement system and reduction of contracted purchasing. Finally, in the late 1980s and early 1990s, the third wave was aimed at liberalizing commodity prices and financial markets.

After the first wave of reform, China's agricultural production growth was abnormally high for a few years due to one-time productivity gains from improved incentives. The success of the 1978 institutional changes in terms of enhancing China's agricultural productivity are well known (McMillan, Whalley, and Zhu 1989; Carter and Zhong 1991a; Fan 1991; Lin 1992; Putterman 1993). However, subsequent agricultural development during the second and third waves of reform in the 1980s and early 1990s has not been without policy problems.

---

2 China's official definition of grain includes rice, corn, wheat, barley, sorghum, millet, soybeans, potatoes, and other coarse grains. Potatoes are converted to a grain equivalent using a conversion ratio of 5:1.

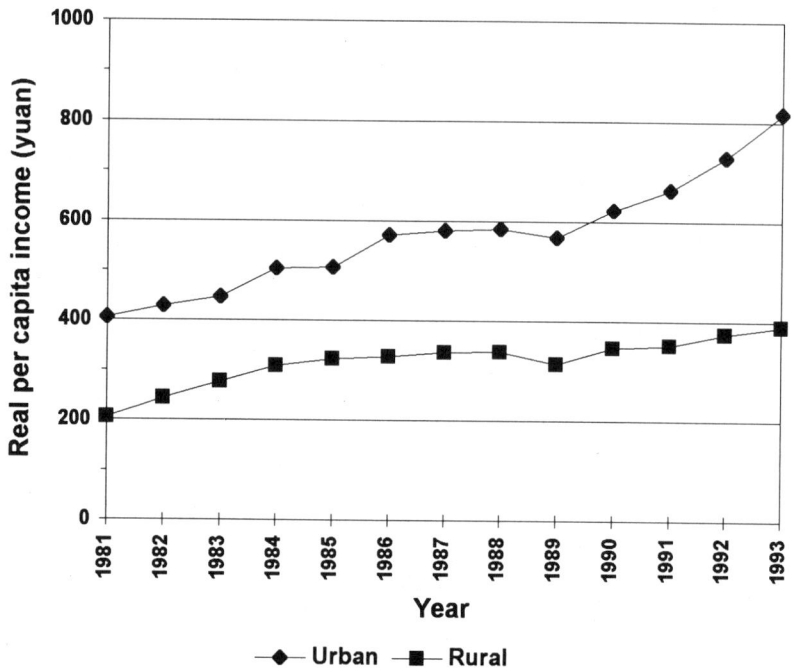

*Figure 2. Urban versus rural per capita incomes: 1981–1993.
Source:* Statistical Yearbook of China, *1994 (SSB, 1994).*

The second and third waves of reform have been unsuccessful in liberalizing the markets for grains and cotton. In fact, the government began a policy retrenchment program for the major grains and cotton in 1989 that is still ongoing. There was a temporary reversal in 1993, when the government announced a new policy entitled "freeing the price while fixing the quantity." However, grain and cotton were brought back under tighter state control later that year, and in 1994 fixed procurement quota prices were reintroduced against farmers' wishes, retail price ceilings were reintroduced in some urban areas, and exports of rice and corn were curtailed in an attempt to control prices. The compulsory procurement of cotton and grain provides the central government with a convenient instrument for imposing (indirect) taxes on agriculture.[3] As a result of this taxation strategy, production incentives have faltered, farm incomes have

---

3 In this context, *taxation* is not defined as the use of income and property taxes. Rather, it refers to government policy that results in a downward bias of domestic agricultural prices relative to nonagricultural prices. The lowering of domestic (relative) agricultural prices places an indirect tax on agriculture and biases the domestic *terms of trade* against agriculture in favor of manufacturing.

stagnated, and the gap between urban and rural incomes has widened once again (see Figure 2). Indeed, China's urban-rural income gap is much wider than anywhere else in Asia (Lardy 1994).

China's policymakers are obsessed with domestic grain output, and it is an understatement to say that the domestic balance of long-term supply and demand for grains is a politically sensitive issue in China. At one extreme pole of the supply demand estimates, it has been estimated that China may need to import about 216 million metric tons (mmt) of grain by the year 2030 (Brown et al. 1995, p. 19), which is an amount greater than total world trade in grains today! The extremely large deficit (216 mmt) is based on the calculation made by Brown et al. that China will experience a 20 percent drop in grain production by the year 2030. Alternatively, China's Ministry of Agriculture has estimated that China will continue to be able to feed itself by the year 2030, at which time the country's population will reach about 1.6 billion (a 400 million increase) and total domestic grain demand will be an estimated 640 mmt.[4] Huang, Rozelle, and Rosegrant (1995) provide alternative estimates of China's grain supply demand balance. They argue that the predicted high level of imports suggested by Brown et al. is possible under certain scenarios, but highly unlikely. Crook (1994a) offers a thoughtful and convincing critique of the Brown et al. projection and asserts that China will not come to depend on huge grain and meat imports.

In China, grain production is relatively land-intensive compared to many other agricultural products (e.g., cotton, sugar, fruits, tobacco, and vegetables), which are more labor-intensive.[5] Hence, the comparative advantage of grain production in China is questionable. In the long run, China will most likely develop an increasing grain deficit due to the combined factors of rising domestic incomes, a growing population, and a declining sown acreage. As discussed

---

4 See the *Journal of Commerce and Commercial* (May 12, 1995, p. 2B) for a report on the Ministry of Agriculture's 1995 study. The study was conducted partly in response to the widely publicized prediction of Brown et al. The results of the ministry's study were presented at a conference celebrating the fiftieth anniversary of the United Nations Food and Agriculture Organization (FAO) in Quebec, Canada, in late 1995. Personal interviews at the ministry revealed that their major disagreement with the work of Brown et al. was over the forecast of a decrease in total grain production in China. In fact, the Ministry of Agriculture's estimate of the growth of grain demand was very similar to that of Brown et al., according to whom the amount of arable land will decline fairly rapidly and the potential to improve fertility on existing land is limited. Alternatively, the Ministry of Agriculture believes that yields on existing land can be improved with more investment and an increase in the multiple-cropping index. Furthermore, the ministry points out that officially reported land area has been underreported in the past, so yields have been overreported (see n. 4 on page 35 for a discussion of the problem of underreported land).

5 Relative to most cash crops, grain is more land-intensive because, per unit of land, the production of grain requires fewer units of labor than the production of cash crops.

in detail in this book, the size of the deficit depends on policy developments related to labor markets, the rural economic structure, investment in agriculture, and domestic food markets. The size of the deficit may also depend on exogenous developments in the international grain market. However, it is doubtful that the deficit will approach anywhere near the level predicted by Brown et al. China will not starve the rest of the world in the coming generation.

The major issues facing further development of China's agricultural sector include the following:

- the apparent slowdown of agricultural productivity growth,
- the lack of properly functioning markets for farm products and farm inputs,
- excess labor in agriculture and the rising gap between rural and urban incomes,
- the slowdown of rural light industries' (i.e., TVEs) absorption of labor; and
- capital outflows from agriculture to rural light industry and urban industry.

The central thesis of this book is that the rural economy is not well integrated with the urban economy, and this will further retard economic growth of rural incomes. Economic policies remain biased against agriculture, as is reflected in the domestic terms of trade. This biased policy is manifest in low incomes for farmers and disinvestment in the agricultural sector. On average, urban incomes are more than double rural ones, and there are serious regional income inequities. Rural income growth in the central and hinterland provinces has slowed. Government expenditure on agriculture has fallen in real terms, and, as a result, the agricultural infrastructure, including research and irrigation systems, has deteriorated. It is doubtful that the agricultural sector can continue to be taxed in order to support a high growth rate in the industrial sector.

The following chapter provides a background description of major developments in China's agricultural policy since reform. The subsequent five chapters address, respectively, the five major issues identified in the paragraph above. The book concludes with a summary section.

Key Findings and Recommendations

The key findings of this book can be summarized by the following policy recommendations:

- China's government should invest more heavily in agriculture and implement land-use reform to encourage private investment. There has been a decline in public investment in agriculture in the post-reform period. Meanwhile, uncertainty over land tenure and low returns to agriculture have resulted in little private investment. As a result, agricultural output growth has slowed down since 1985. Future productivity gains could be realized in crop and livestock production through renewed investment in infrastructure, irrigation, and research.

- China's government should work to set up a modern marketing infrastructure to facilitate the functioning of private open markets for key agricultural products such as grain and cotton. This should be followed up with a complete liberalization of these markets. The slowdown in grain and cotton output growth over the past decade was partly due to a failure of government policies to free up markets for these products.
- China's farmers have become discouraged by low profitability. Government procurement of major farm products has been used to extract profits from agriculture for industrialization purposes. This implicit taxation of agriculture has induced additional capital outflows out of agriculture through the rural financial system. The government should reverse this situation and strive to raise the profit incentives for farmers.
- The labor market should be freed up. An important division remains between the rural and urban economies, as is evidenced by the large gap between rural and urban incomes. This division is due mainly to the immobility of labor. Reform of the resident registration system (the *hukou* system) is required. If combined with elimination of subsidies to the urban sector (e.g., cheap housing), this will help lead to integration of the rural–urban economies.
- The government should abolish its regional and national self-sufficiency policies with regard to food production and initiate intraprovincial and international agricultural trade liberalization. This strategy would allow farmers in each region to produce according to their comparative advantage and would lead to income gains. Liberalizing intraprovincial trade would also contribute toward better integration of the rural–urban economies and help solve the problem of excess rural labor.
- The central government should discontinue the disproportionate emphasis that it places on the economic well-being of urban residents compared to rural residents. The government overemphasizes the importance of keeping urban food prices low. This emphasis is unnecessary because grains have a relatively low share of the urban household budget. Because of the importance attached to keeping urban prices low, fluctuation of commodity prices induces costly policy reversals, which undermine the credibility of the government with regard to agricultural policy.

CHAPTER 2

Major Policy Developments in Agriculture

Basic Features of the Reform

It is generally accepted that China's central government never intended the 1978 reforms to be comprehensive and long lasting. The reforms were not well planned in advance. To begin with, the reform policies were aimed at overcoming the adverse economic effects of the Cultural Revolution, through reinstituting material incentives in rural areas to stimulate production within the existing political and social framework. After a few years, the initial success encouraged the government to adopt bolder reform measures and finally led to the formal announcement of the transformation of the whole economy into a "socialist market economy."

Communal farming was the first institution to be reformed. Rural communes were established in the late 1950s as the basic institution in rural China, and the communes were largely designed to be self-sufficient in food production. The system of communes lasted just over twenty years. Immediately prior to their termination, a typical commune consisted of ten to fifteen production brigades, with each brigade further divided into about ten production teams of twenty to thirty households each. The commune was both a government body and a compulsory cooperative, carrying out directives from higher levels of the government and managing small-scale enterprises and shops. The brigades not only passed down directives and allocated quotas, but they also operated primary schools, clinics, and shops. Under the brigades, the production teams were the basic unit of organization responsible for agricultural production, accounting, and income distribution. The government established a monopolistic-monopsonistic procurement and marketing system for most agricultural outputs and inputs, and centralized sown-area plans were implemented.

The crisis caused by the Great Leap Forward and its aftermath (1959-61) placed some early pressure on the central planning of agriculture, and soon afterwards, some limited economic experiments were begun that linked remuneration to the quantity and type of work. Although the official position of the government was that of encouraging remuneration experiments, it was on the condition that collective ownership and management should be maintained. The so-called *Da Baogan* or *Baogan Dao Hu* system that was secretly adopted by farmers in some locations in Anhui Province in 1978 was first tried in the mid-1950s. It was used again in the early 1960s, and later became known as the household responsibility system (HRS). The HRS is a type of private farming system, with property rights divided between ownership (by the team or village) and management (by the households). This system contracts out, to individual farm households, land-use rights, production and procurement quotas, and, in some cases, part of the fixed assets of the production team. After fulfilling quota obligations and submitting a certain amount of total output or revenue to the team for collective purposes, the individual farmer can keep the remainder.

By as late as 1980, the government still insisted on a certain degree of collective management in farming and reluctantly accepted the HRS as an inevitable measure in poor, remote, and mountainous regions, or in places where farmers had lost all confidence in collective management. However, this policy changed rather quickly, and the HRS was openly encouraged in 1981-82.[1] Direct control over production and sown-area plans was loosened, and indirect control through procurement and marketing then became a major tool in government planning. By the mid-1980s, unified procurement was abandoned, a two-track price system was adopted, farmers were allowed to sell more of their products in free markets,[2] and market forces slowly entered the resource allocation process. The state's role declined continuously until 1994, when it suddenly resurged. Today, key food items are still subject to both procurement quotas and fixed prices.

When the communal system was abolished in the mid-1980s, townships and villages inherited some of the functions that had previously been performed by the communes and production brigades. Formally, the townships and villages were government or administrative bodies, but they also acted as managers of

---

1 See Ash (1993) and Sicular (1988, 1993) for further descriptions of the agriculture reform.
2 Free markets began to develop for fruits, vegetables, and meat even in the early 1980s.

the collective property left by the communal system. Individual farmers signed HRS contracts with the village. Procurement quotas, taxes, and other obligations to the state and local government were allocated by the township and village, according to land size and family size. In many cases, these small communities established and now operate township and village enterprises (TVEs). The TVEs provide some subsidies to agriculture,[3] and support social welfare programs. The townships and villages are responsible for primary and/or high school education and basic health care within their jurisdiction.

The current township (*xiang*) and village (*cun*) organizational structure constitutes the local government for farmers. In 1993, the average number of households in a township was 4,770 (*Statistical Yearbook of China* [SSB, 1994]). At the township level, the party committee is in charge and the township government carries out routine administrative duties, such as allocating procurement quotas, enforcing the implementation of the quota, and collecting taxes. In addition, the township government oversees the running of township enterprises and provides hospitals and high schools. The head of the township government is usually a member of the party committee. The economic cooperatives at the township level provide financial services, agricultural input supplies, and services related to the marketing of output.

The village is roughly equivalent to the former production brigades and usually consists of about 286 households (as of 1993). A branch of the township party committee is in charge of the village. The village committee has functions similar to the township government, but on a smaller scale, such as managing village enterprises and providing health clinics and elementary schools. The village committees have some economic co-ops, but not as many as at the township level. For instance, a village rarely has a financial co-op. Recently, the central government has encouraged the townships and villages to play a greater role in agricultural production, such as providing certain types of farming services under contracts with individual farmers. In southern China, the TVEs actually continue to act as water allocation managers or coordinators, and hence as informal production planners, at least for some crop production.

Finally, the *cunmin xiaozu* is the equivalent of the former production team, and consists of about twenty to thirty households. They own the land,[4] contract out land-use rights to individual households, and pass on a share of the mandatory procurement quotas to the individual households. They are also re-

---

3 Lin (1995, p. 20) reports that farmers in the coastal provinces will produce grain only if they are provided with large production subsidies from the TVEs. See Chapter 6 for a discussion of the TVE subsidies to agriculture.
4 According to the constitution, the *cunmin xiaozu* owns the land, but in practice the central government establishes the length of land leases. Currently the leases are for thirty years.

sponsible for distributing tax obligations to each household. In some areas, the *cunmin xiaozu* provides machinery services and custom work.

With their newfound decision-making power under the HRS, farmers responded to favorable prices by boosting production with available technology. From 1979 through 1993, the gross value of agricultural output (GVAO) increased at an annual rate of 6.1 percent, compared with an annual average of 2.7 percent for the previous twenty-six years (1952 through 1977).[5] Table 1 reports average annual growth rates for China's GVAO from 1979–93 and two subperiods (1979–84 and 1985–93), and for the five main components of GVAO: cropping, forestry, animal husbandry, sideline production,[6] and fisheries. Cropping and animal husbandry are by far the two most important components, accounting for 59 percent and 26 percent of GVAO, respectively, in 1990. From 1979 to 1984, the total value of agricultural output grew rapidly at 7.7 percent per year. Among the five components of GVAO, sideline production and animal husbandry were the fastest-growing sectors, with annual growth rates of 15.5 percent and 9.7 percent, respectively. The cropping sector grew at an annual rate of 6.9 percent in real terms. Average annual growth in production fell significantly after 1984, and the decline to the lowest growth rate occurred in the cropping sector.

Measured by sown area, grain production is the largest component in the cropping sector, with about 74 percent of sown area. About 32 percent of the gross value of agricultural output is attributed to grain production. (Refer to Table 2, where growth rates for grain output, sown area, and yield are reported.) Although its share of sown area declined from 80 to 74 percent during the last fifteen years, grain production increased from 304.8 mmt in 1978 to 444.5 mmt in 1994 (a 45 percent increase in total, or 2.3 percent annually). However, the growth rate was much higher during the first six years of reform. The summary statistics on yield growth in the last two rows of Table 2 suggest that grain productivity may have slowed, as growth in average yields declined from 5.5 percent during 1978–84, to 1.7 percent during 1985–94.

China is the world's largest producer and consumer of grain, with rice, wheat, and corn being the principal grains. In order to feed 1.2 billion people, China devotes more than 30 percent of its labor force to grain production. China's farmers constantly face political pressure to increase the nation's grain supply, and this pressure is created by a large, densely settled population and a limited amount of cultivated land per capita. Yields have been maximized by using high levels of inputs and by increasing the number of crops harvested per

---

[5] These figures, and many others in this book, were obtained from the *Statistical Yearbook of China* (State Statistical Bureau [SSB]), various issues.
[6] China's Statistical Bureau defines "sideline production" as activities that include gathering and hunting, family handicrafts, and the like.

Table 1. Real Growth Rates (%) of Gross Value of Agricultural Output, 1979–1993

Year	GVAO	Cropping	Forestry	Animal Husbandry	Sideline Production	Fisheries
1979	7.5	7.2	1.4	14.6	−3.5	−3.4
1980	1.4	−0.5	2.2	7.0	6.1	7.7
1981	5.8	5.9	4.1	5.9	24.0	4.4
1982	11.3	10.3	9.5	13.2	21.9	12.3
1983	7.8	8.3	10.2	3.9	11.6	8.6
1984	12.3	9.9	19.0	13.4	33.0	17.6
1985	3.4	−2.0	4.5	17.2	20.6	18.9
1986	3.4	0.9	−3.6	5.5	20.0	20.5
1987	5.8	5.3	−0.3	3.2	15.4	18.1
1988	3.9	−0.2	2.3	12.7	12.6	11.6
1989	3.1	1.8	0.4	5.6	6.0	7.2
1990	7.6	8.6	3.1	7.0	3.8	10.0
1991	3.7	1.0	8.0	8.9	0.3	7.6
1992	6.4	3.5	7.7	8.8	11.2	15.3
1993	7.8	5.2	8.0	10.8	n.a.	18.4
Average growth rate (%)						
1979–93	6.1	4.3	5.1	9.2	13.1	11.7
1979–84	7.7	6.9	7.7	9.7	15.5	7.9
1985–93	5.0	2.7	3.3	8.9	11.2	14.2
Share of GVAO (%)						
1979	100	75	4	17	3	1
1990	100	59	4	26	6	5

Source: *Statistical Yearbook of China* (SSB, 1993 and 1994).

unit of cultivated land. Historically, substantial technological advances have been made in China's grain production. Sophisticated seed breeding, water control, land preparation, and fertilizer-using technologies have a long history of development in the country.

The 1978 policy reform had two initial components: higher prices and greater freedom of farmers to make production decisions. The price of government-procured grain, on average, was raised only 17.5 percent during the thirteen years prior to the reforms, but there was an almost 20 percent increase in prices in 1979 alone. However, even after the price hikes, China's farmers were still receiving less than the world price for their grain. At the same time, the

Table 2. Grain Production in China, 1978–1994

Year	Grain output (mmt)	Grain sown area (mil. ha)	Grain yield (kg/ha)
1978	304.8	120.6	2,596.0
1979	332.1	119.3	2,784.8
1980	320.6	117.2	2,734.5
1981	325.0	115.0	2,827.5
1982	354.5	113.5	3,124.4
1983	387.3	114.0	3,396.0
1984	407.3	112.9	3,608.3
1985	379.1	108.8	3,483.2
1986	391.5	110.9	3,529.3
1987	403.0	111.3	3,622.0
1988	394.1	110.1	3,578.6
1989	407.6	112.2	3,632.4
1990	446.2	113.5	3,933.0
1991	435.3	112.3	3,875.8
1992	442.7	110.6	4,003.8
1993	456.5	110.5	4,130.8
1994	444.5	109.3	4,066.8
Average growth rate (%)			
1978–84	4.8	−1.1	5.5
1985–94	1.8	0.05	1.7

Note: The central government has officially indicated that arable land is underreported by about 20 percent (Crook 1993b). The grain sown area probably has been underreported as well. This means that yields have been overreported. However, this discrepancy has existed since the mid-1950s, and thus the error may have been constant from year to year.
Source: *Statistical Yearbook of China* (SSB, 1994).

central government continued to emphasize both national and regional self-sufficiency in grains (especially in rice, wheat, and corn) and maintained control over mandatory grain procurement and grain reserves. Although the grain market was to be "freed" in the early 1990s, attempts to do so have been unsuccessful; recently, the central government has moved backward with regard to grain-policy reform, and has reimposed large mandatory procurement quotas with regard to rice and wheat across the country, and soybeans and corn in the northeast provinces. The components of the mandatory procurement quotas vary across provinces. Grains such as potatoes, peas, and sorghum are not as tightly controlled by the government, and the production and consumption of these grains responds to market forces. However, other minor grains, such as millet, beans, barley, and oats are controlled in those provinces where the production of these crops is relatively important.

The rural township and village enterprises (TVEs) and other nonfarm rural activities were developed along with the agricultural sector. The growth of TVEs exceeded all expectations, as their total output value accounted for 66 percent of total rural output value and 32 percent of total output value of society by 1992. Measured by value of output, rural TVEs and other nonagricultural rural activities are about twice as large as traditional agriculture.

The TVEs were encouraged by the government with tax exemptions for the first two profitable years, and then with a 50 percent reduction in income tax for the following three years. The government also allocated, through the state banks, loans to TVEs, which had been available only to state enterprises during the early stages of reform. These "planned" loans had low nominal interest rates, and sometimes negative real rates of interest. The government's intention was explained by the slogan *yi gong bu nong* ("subsidizing agriculture with industry"). The government hoped that farmers would earn off-farm income from the TVEs and cross-subsidize their farming activities with profit generated from TVEs. In those cases where TVEs were farmer-owned collective enterprises, the TVEs often subsidized those farmers remaining in the cropping sector. This will be explained in greater detail later.

The share of the labor force employed in the agricultural sector declined from 70 percent of the national total in 1978 to less than 60 percent in 1993. Agriculture in China is relatively labor-intensive, and because labor is not entirely free to move about, the 60 percent share of agricultural employment in the total employment is far greater than agriculture's share of the GDP (which is only about 20 percent). The agricultural sector's contribution to fiscal revenue is quite small, if measured in total direct taxes collected from the sector. In 1991, the total amount of agricultural tax collected was 9 billion yuan, or 3 percent of the total tax revenues in that year. But this figure seriously underestimates agriculture's real contribution to fiscal revenue. The artificially low prices set for farm products are used by the government to keep wages low in the urban areas and to turn agricultural surplus into industrial profit.

Stages of Economic Reform

China's economic reforms can be divided into three chronological stages: 1978–84, 1985–88, and 1989–present. The first stage (1978–84) was a period in which reforms were focused primarily on agriculture, and agriculture's growth was rapid. During the second stage (1985–88), urban reforms were also initiated, and these led to overheated industrial growth (primarily the TVEs)

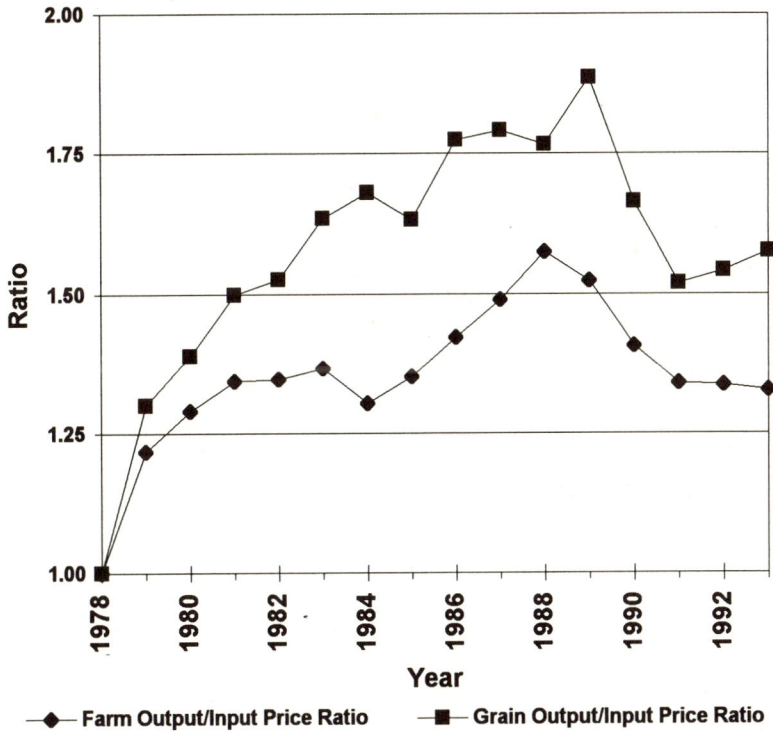

Figure 3. Ratio of farm output prices to input prices: 1978–1993. Note: The farm output price index is the overall weighted farm output price index; the grain output price index is the purchasing price index; and, the input price index is for agricultural producer goods.
Source: Compiled from the Statistical Yearbook of China, *1994 (SSB, 1994)*.

and double-digit inflation. In agriculture, policy reform during the second stage focused on liberalizing the mandatory procurement system, except for grain and cotton. The third stage (1989–present) is a period characterized by speedy reforms outside of agriculture, following Deng Xiaoping's visit to the southern provinces in 1992. In agriculture, the government eliminated urban food subsidies and attempted (unsuccessfully) to liberalize the grain markets.

The First Stage (1978–1984)

In the agricultural sector, procurement prices were increased by over 20 percent in 1979 (see Figure 3), and the above-quota price premiums were also raised. Centralized sown-area plans were relaxed to a certain extent, and procurement quotas were gradually reduced, and even abolished for some commodities. Various production responsibility systems were tried, and finally the HRS became the dominant form. Rural markets were formally reopened to give farmers the opportunity to trade their surplus goods after fulfilling quota delivery obligations, and private long-distance shipping and marketing were permitted.

Stimulated by these policy measures, and supported by available technology (such as hybrid rice) and an enhanced supply of manufactured inputs, production of grain increased from 304.8 to 407.3 mmt during the first stage, equivalent to an annual growth rate of 4.8 percent over the six years. Cotton increased even faster, 19.3 percent annually, from 2.17 to 6.26 mmt. Oil-bearing crops increased at a rate of 14.7 percent, from 5.22 to 11.91 metric tons. During the same period, meat (including pork, beef, and mutton) production increased from 8.56 to 15.41 mmt, while aquatic production increased from 4.66 to 6.19 mmt. The annual growth rates were 10.3 and 4.8 percent, respectively, for the meat and aquatic subsectors.

The GVAO increased from 139.7 to 321.4 billion yuan, in nominal terms, in six years. In real terms, it increased at an impressive rate of 7.7 percent per annum. The real annual growth rates of the five subsectors—cropfarming, forestry, animal husbandry, sideline production, and fisheries—were 6.9, 7.7, 9.7, 15.5, and 7.9 percent, respectively. By 1984, cropfarming's share in GVAO declined to 68 percent from 77 percent in 1978, while those of all other subsectors increased.

The Second Stage (1984–1988)

The great achievements of the initial reforms for the rural areas encouraged the government to adopt bolder measures to reform the urban sector. Major policy measures in the mid-1980s included double-track pricing, enterprise tax and wage reforms, banking and financial reform, revenue-sharing systems between central and local governments, and the opening up of fourteen coastal cities, in addition to the special economic zones established in the previous stage. Although the urban sector benefited significantly in this period, it suffered from double-digit inflation in 1988. However, the agricultural sector, especially the cropping subsector, was adversely influenced by policies implemented during this time.

The government did not raise urban retail food prices during the early 1980s, even in the face of rising procurement prices. According to the 1990 *Price Statistical Yearbook of China*, retail grain prices in urban state shops increased by 6.3 percent from 1978 to 1980, and by 9.9 percent from 1980 to 1985. These are weighted averages and basically reflected changes in composition, not price changes. At the same time, farm-gate quota prices had doubled, and negotiated prices more than doubled. As a result, urban food subsidies reached one-fourth of the total government budget during this period. Per capita food consumption soared, especially for meats (see Figure 1). The budgetary burden associated with the urban food subsidies became excessive, restricting the government's ability to allocate more of its budget to industrial investment. The situation became critical with the record-breaking harvest of 1984, which resulted in a large surplus of grain and cotton, and associated problems with storing the surplus. In an attempt to ameliorate the situation, the government converted the thirty-year-old procurement system into a so-called contracted purchasing system, with newly established *unified* prices equal to the weighted average of the former quota and above-quota prices. The marginal price was now the *unified* price instead of the above-quota price, and thus the marginal price for grain was effectively reduced by 35 percent.[7] In addition, the quantity of cotton purchased by the central government was reduced in both 1985 and 1986. The government cut its purchases by 25 percent in 1985. Historically, the government had been the only buyer of cotton, and thus the farmers responded by reducing both grain- and cotton-sown areas, as well as the application of manufactured inputs. As a result, grain production decreased by 7 percent in 1985, and cotton by 34 percent.

As grain did not reach the 1984 production level again until 1989, the government soon announced that its purchasing contracts with farmers were "state contracts." Hence, the delivery quotas were still compulsory, and sales onto the free market were allowed only after fulfillment of quota obligations. Purchase prices for major crops were raised again, and the government again relied on sown area and procurement plans, through local cadres in somewhat informal ways. These policy measures led to resources being reallocated toward grain production and, in many regions, away from activities for which the subsector had a comparative advantage because of higher labor productivity in nongrain farming activities.

During this time period, the industrial sector grew rapidly, but grain and cotton production stagnated. Grain production was 394.1 mmt in 1988, which was 3.2 percent lower than the 1984 level. Cotton output was maintained at 4.15 mmt in 1988, as in 1985, and was 33.7 percent lower than in 1984. Oil-bearing crops increased at a rate of 2.8 percent and meat production increased at 9.2 percent.

The GVAO reached 586.5 billion yuan by 1988. However, the real growth rate from 1985–88 was 4.1 percent per year, much smaller than the 7.6 percent registered in the previous period (1978–84). Structural change in the agricul-

---

[7] Economists refer to one additional unit sold as the "marginal" unit. Therefore, the marginal price is the price of an extra unit of grain sold.

tural sector was more dramatic, as crop farming and forestry grew at only 0.96 and 0.68 percent, respectively, whereas animal husbandry increased at 9.51 percent, and sideline production and fisheries increased at 17.1 and 17.2 percent, respectively. Crop-farming's share in the GVAO declined further, from 63 percent in 1985 to 56 percent in 1988.

The Third Stage (1988–Present)

The reform measures adopted in the second stage were quite successful in boosting industrial growth in urban areas, but they also led to double-digit inflation by 1988. To slow down the inflation rate, the government postponed further reforms of the price system, recentralized control over prices for many items, tightened the money supply and credit, and cut, or postponed, investment in a wide range of projects under the "rectification program" (see International Monetary Fund 1993). As a result, the whole economy grew at an annual rate of 9.36 percent (in real GNP) during the 1988–94 time period, lower than the 10.05 percent achieved over the previous ten years, and the 10.38 percent over the 1985–88 time period.

Notably, the agricultural sector recovered somewhat in this time period. Measured in comparable prices, the GVAO increased by 43.3 percent in 1994 over 1988, or 6.18 percent annually. Major farm products, which were of particular concern to the government, all increased significantly. Grain production reached a new peak of 446.3 mmt in 1990, 13.2 percent higher than in 1988. The year 1993 witnessed another new record grain crop of 456.5 mmt. On average, grain production was 438.9 mmt per year during the 1988–94 time period, 19.9 percent higher than over the 1984–88 time period. Cotton production was 5.68 mmt in 1991, 36.9 percent higher than in 1988. Although it declined somewhat afterward, cotton production in the 1988–94 time period was always higher than in 1988, except in 1993. The average production was 10.2 percent higher in this time period than in the previous one. Animal and aquatic production continued to increase during the 1988–94 time period. Meat production increased from 24.8 mmt in 1988 to 44.99 mmt in 1994, almost doubling in six years; milk and aquatic products increased from 4.19 to 6.09 and from 106.1 to 214.3 mmt, respectively.

In contrast to the previous stage, economic development and reform both picked up again in the third stage. Although the government had already taken some measures in late 1990 to bring the economy back from low growth during the retrenchment period, it formally declared an end to the rectification program in early 1992. Later that year, when it was announced that the socialist market economy was being set as a goal for the country, the process of reform once again accelerated, with a definite objective to establish a market-oriented economic system, including restructuring the role and function of the government.

Agricultural marketing was further liberalized in the first part of this period. The retail prices for grain and edible oil rations in the urban areas were raised by 20.9 percent in 1991 and another 39.2 percent in 1992, bringing the rationed retail price equal to the procurement price and leaving the government to subsidize only the associated marketing costs. By the end of 1993, almost all cities and counties abandoned the rationing system, and the state-run grain shops in the urban areas started conducting business as commercial enterprises. On the producer side, the government announced the end of fixed prices for "contracted purchasing" in 1993. Though farmers were still obliged to sell a specified quantity (quota) of grain to the government, the price was to be at the market level. As before, selling onto the free market was allowed once delivery obligations had been fulfilled.

However, the government failed to specify what market price should be used for procurement purposes and by what date farmers had to fulfill their delivery obligations. The vagueness of this policy created problems for both producers and consumers. When faced with another run of rapid inflation, farmers withheld grain deliveries in the fall and winter of 1993–94, anticipating higher prices. Local governments in surplus areas responded by prohibiting outward grain shipments to enforce the "quota delivery first" policy, but the real objective was to reduce their procurement expenditures. This contributed to a substantial escalation in grain retail prices in urban areas. The government reintroduced urban retail price controls and, in many regions, a fixed purchasing price for grain.

The market price increases in late 1993 and the decline of grain production in 1994 were viewed by the government as signals that more administrative control was necessary. After that it was announced and/or reemphasized, at the end of 1994, that the government channel was the only one in cotton marketing, that nongovernmental agencies were not allowed to buy grain directly from farmers, especially when the contracted purchasing quota had not yet been fulfilled, and that government agencies should prevail in the grain market. A "temporary blockade" on rice and corn exports was imposed in late 1994 and, in addition, all provincial governors were made personally responsible for grain production and supply under their jurisdiction, and prices were not to be raised without central permission.[8]

China's central government is now facing a difficult policy dilemma. The experience over the past fifteen years clearly indicates that market-oriented reform is the major force driving economic and agricultural growth. However, the

---

8 Refer to Chapter 4, "The Role of Markets," for further discussion of the government decision to apply greater administrative control.

government was reluctant to give up on the long-term development strategy of pursuing industrialization at the cost of agriculture. A low-cost supply of grain and cotton is at the core of this strategy, and administrative measures were consistently used to achieve this goal, unless a crisis made a price increase the only way to stimulate production.

Driving provincial governors to increase grain production, while at the same time prohibiting price increases, is clearly a setback of reform. It is uncertain how long the setback will last, and it is also uncertain that the provincial governors will strictly follow the central policy, as it is likely to hurt the local economies.

Other General Issues Associated with Agricultural Reform

Environmental Effects

The initial effects of reform on natural resources and the environment were quite positive in the late 1970s and early 1980s. As diversification in agricultural production was permitted and local autonomy was recognized, the forced farming on marginal land (such as on hillsides with steep slopes) was stopped, and the land was returned to its natural and best uses, such as grazing or forestry. Simultaneously, when the pressure to increase grain-sown area was reduced, farmers in southern China responded with a reduction in triple- and/or double-cropping. The decrease in farming intensity not only reduced the marginal cost of grain production but also improved the fertility and chemical conditions of the soil.

One negative event associated with the HRS took place in the western mountainous areas in the early 1980s, where poor farmers cut trees on collectively owned and state-owned lands. Similar incidents had occurred earlier, when trees had been cut and used as fuel to produce steel during the Great Leap Forward (1958–61) and when lakes and hilly areas had been turned into farmland during the Cultural Revolution (1966–76). Unlike the two earlier "planned" and organized movements, however, the cutting of trees in the early 1980s was done for individual farmers' interests and was against government policies and regulations. Fortuitously for the farmers, local authorities were reluctant to intervene, because of the lack of a clear division of property rights among different levels of governments, and the dissolution of the communes.

Another major problem with the HRS was the sharp decline in investment in water projects and other infrastructure facilities. Every year, during the commune era, millions of workers were mobilized to work on new irrigation and drainage projects, or on maintenance of old ones; this was crucial to the success of the labor-intensive farming and provided protection against bad weather.

When the communal system was replaced by the HRS, no alternative institution was established in this regard, nor did the state intervene through increased public investment.[9] As a result, the existing facilities deteriorated, and this partly contributed to the decline in output in the cropping sector around 1985.

Industrial pollution is a serious problem for agriculture. Pollution of air, water, and land from urban industry was quite serious even before China's economic reforms were launched. Since implementation of the reforms, increasing industrial pollution in the rural areas associated with the development of TVEs has caused much concern (Guo 1994). The TVEs are no longer necessarily engaged in processing farm products. In fact, their industrial structure is quite similar to that of urban enterprises. Because the TVEs are scattered throughout rural China (in nearly every village in many parts of the country), pollution is also widespread, affecting vast amounts of farmland. The TVEs expend less effort than urban enterprises on fighting pollution, and unfortunately there is little incentive for local authorities to enforce the existing regulations and standards.

Since the mid-1980s, the central government has shown greater interest in natural resource and environmental issues. Several laws have been passed by the National People's Congress, or its standing committee, in the areas of utilization and conservation of land, water, and forestry. This is consistent with the restructuring of the role and function of the state and is likely to yield positive effects in the long run. However, as no institution has been established to mobilize resources for public project purposes, and as the state has not increased its investment in infrastructure supporting agriculture, the capacity of agriculture to withstand natural disasters is likely to decline further.

Farm Size

One major concern that immediately emerged following the establishment of the HRS was the fragmentation of farms. According to Lin (1995), economies of scale were sacrificed in the household-based system, but the gains from the superior incentive structure of that system more than compensated for economies of scale losses from elimination of the previous team system. For example, when households became independent producers in the mid-1980s, a typical 18-hectare (ha)[10] farm was broken into about thirty smaller farms, and each of these thirty were further fragmented into four or five tiny sections, scattered in different locations. Although production incentives increased with

---

9 However, in the mid 1980s the government instituted the corvee labor system, which required rural residents to spend fifteen to twenty days a year on public works, such as roads and irrigation.
10 One hectare is equivalent to 2.47 acres.

the HRS, losses in efficiencies associated with farm size and land fragmentation were recognized as a problem, prompting several measures to be taken at the local level. One strategy enacted was land reconsolidation, which aimed to reduce the number of plots farmed by one household, but it did not enlarge the size of farms as a whole. This attempt at consolidation threatened farmers' confidence in land leases and often led to conflicts among households. This measure gave farmers permission to subcontract among themselves to consolidate plots.

The second measure, related to farm organization, was the introduction of the two-tier management system. Under this system, a household was responsible for its production as before, while the community (village) arranged and provided services such as machinery operation and consolidated pest control. The arrangement could also be extended to supplying inputs and marketing outputs. Though this two-tier management system might have lowered costs within the HRS framework, it did not address the problem of small farm size.

The third local-level measure was the establishment of "specialized production associations." These associations were mainly organized for certain types of cash crops or small animal production units, providing technical services to their members, and often marketing products on the behalf of members. Unlike the two-tier management system, these associations engaged in both production and marketing, and were not restricted to local communities such as villages.

A key issue associated with further reform is whether the barrier to free migration of labor, both interregionally and from rural to urban areas, will be removed. Under the current situation, most farmers will not give up their land, which is viewed as security. A critical barrier is the resident registration system (the *hukou* system), which assigns different legal status to rural and urban inhabitants and dictates the location in which individuals live and work. A proposal to reform the system was made public in March 1994, but it is unclear whether there will be any meaningful developments. Another barrier, perhaps more important, is the actual discrimination in employment, housing, and access to public utility facilities in the urban areas. Although urban enterprises now are willing to hire more workers who lack formal resident status, they experience difficulty in doing so because the current access to housing and public utility services is designed to benefit only formal urban residents. In direct opposition to the proposal to reform the resident registration system, many city governments are now tightening their control on inward migration of rural labor. For example, enterprises are charged extra fees (according to the number of hired rural laborers), to compensate for the cost burden of increased public utility services. In addition, city governments have issued orders for urban enterprises formally to set employment priorities. Since 1994, transient rural workers who seek formal urban jobs have been required to obtain "work permits" from both the home county government and the destination city government.

Clearly, further reform of the organization of farms will depend on reforms of the resident registration system, reforms in the urban sector, and a change in the government's attitude of favoritism toward urban residents. All of these factors have been viewed as critical to political stability. Hence, changes are expected to occur only gradually, and on condition that major chaos can be avoided.

Property Rights and Land-Tenure Issues

The most confusing legal issue associated with China's rural reform relates to property rights.[11] Under the communal system, most means of production, including land, were owned by the production teams, while the commune and the production brigade owned and ran schools, clinics, and small nonfarm enterprises. Legally, those assets were the common property of members in the respective organization, and could not be divided or distributed among members. Income was distributed solely according to accumulated work points.

In the early 1980s, farmers signed HRS contracts with the team, as the latter was the formal owner of the land. When the communal system collapsed in the mid-1980s, the reestablished township and village committees, government, and semigovernmental administrative bodies, respectively, were not the legal inheritors of the common property. Under the HRS, the village committee replaced the production team as the manager of the land contract system. However, the central government retained the right to change the time length of land leases at any time.

The common-property nature of the land ensured equal rights to each formal member of the village. This guaranteed an approximately equal distribution of the land (in terms of quantity and quality) among the members. Therefore, fragmentation and frequent redistribution of land following any changes in village population were inevitable. The common-property nature also entitled each member to an equal right to share any returns to the land, sometimes evenly and sometimes based on work performed. If a member left the team or village, he or she lost all rights to share property returns, thus the incentives to make long-term investments were low.

Property rights were not a major issue when farmers had little opportunity to find permanent jobs in the cities and some land only brought negative rights, such as quota obligations, instead of economic returns. However, because seasonal labor migration is now more common in the eastern coastal regions, and as new developments in market reform and industrialization have increased

11 See Prosterman, Hanstad, and Ping (1994) for a recent discussion of problems in the farmland market.

land values in many locations, farmers in some regions have claimed their right to share returns from common property.

An experiment has recently been conducted in Guangdong Province and the areas surrounding Shanghai, apparently originating from local initiatives. The new institution is a share-holding cooperative, in which all assets, including the land, are divided into shares and distributed among existing members. A portion of the net earnings of the properties can be distributed according to shares, and the shares can be transferred, inherited, or returned to the cooperative for monetary compensation.

Some of the same property rights issues exist for those TVEs which are common properties of the township or village. A formal member can enjoy all benefits, including income transfers in the form of either direct payments or subsidies to farm production, and the accumulated assets of the TVEs. But the member may lose these rights once he or she leaves. Some experiments similiar to those being undertaken with the cooperatives are also taking place with TVEs.

For most of China, a current concern is still the duration and transferability of land leases. This impacts long-term investments and economies of scale. The basic issue is whether ownership or the right to use the resource will be privatized in some form. It is a politically sensitive issue in China, and no clear-cut solution is imminent. An equally important issue is the unwillingness of farmers to leave their land, thereby providing an actual supply of land-use rights. Experience from other eastern Asian economies indicates that land transfers will be infrequent, and small farms will continue to be the dominant characteristic in the long run.

Domestic Regional Trade

In general, China's farmers have been forced to be regionally self-sufficient in production of grain, with about 65 percent of grain output being consumed on farms today. However, the domestic grain "trade" has been slowly growing. Prior to reform, farmers provided all other sectors with approximately 50 mmt of grain per year, which accounted for about 20 percent of the total output. Over the 1990–92 time period, the same figures, on average, increased to 140 mmt and 31 percent, respectively. The increase in the internal trade of grain was a result of production growth and diversification. A large portion of the increased supply was likely feed grains. A recent study (S. Wu 1993) reported that interprovincial grain shipments in the 1980s represented about 5 to 10 percent of total domestic trade, ranging from 10 to 20 mmt annually. Usually, the major surplus regions were comprised of the six provinces in the middle and lower reaches of the Chang Jiang (Yangtse) River, two provinces in the northeast (Heilongjiang and Jilin), and two provinces in the middle and lower reaches of the Huang He (Yellow) River (Henan and Shandong). The other provinces and minority autonomous regions were more or less in deficit positions. Rice was shipped out of the Yangtse River region, while the other two surplus regions exported corn, soybean, and wheat.

The study in 1993 by S. Wu also indicated that the domestic grain trade had gone through a major transition. In 1980, the government procured 80 percent of the grain leaving the farms. By 1990, only 36 percent of grain leaving the farm was handled through the compulsory contracted purchasing system, whereas the "negotiated purchasing and marketing companies," subsidiaries of the government procurement agencies, were competing with private business on a commercial basis for the remaining 64 percent. Overall, the state-owned enterprises were still the major traders in the grain market, handling about 85 percent of the wholesale grain and quite a large percentage of the retail trade. However, private businesses in the grain trade were growing rapidly, first in areas of retailing and then in small-scale wholesaling.

The percentage of the domestic grain trade handled by nongovernment businesses is unlikely to be expanded dramatically in the near future. Currently, the central government purchases about 50 mmt per year through mandatory procurement. In addition, it requires government grain bureaus to buy 60 to 70 mmt from the free market. This leaves little room for private trade. There are additional reasons why private trade in grain is limited; these include congestion in all modes of transportation, the underdevelopment of commercial warehouses and communication facilities, and the absence of large farmers' marketing organizations.

In February 1993, the central government announced a new policy for grain procurement, whereby the quantity procured was to be at the "free market" price. Input prices were to be freed up, with a cash subsidy paid to farmers instead of subsidized input prices. In addition, all provincial governments were to be responsible for interprovincial shipments and those shipments were to be at the market price. The grain deficit provinces disagreed with this policy change, as it placed them at a disadvantage; previously, the central government had been responsible for interprovincial shipments, the deficit provinces were able to purchase grain from the central government at a fixed price, and the central government paid part of the marketing costs. However, the system prior to 1993 did not work very well (Lardy 1990). The transition to the new policy was made difficult by the fact that grain prices increased sharply following the 1993 harvest. Surplus provinces reneged on many of the contracts, maintaining that the contracts were "no good" because the price increased after the contract was negotiated. To make matters worse, grain production fell in 1994 by 2.5 percent and the central government overreacted to this small decline in production by stepping up policy retrenchment. The government increased the quantity under mandatory procurement in 1994, and in March 1995 the Peoples Congress formally introduced a system stipulating that provincial governors have the responsibility for provincial grain balances. These measures represent a significant reversal of the previous farm liberalization policy, the consequences of which might be quite detrimental to agricultural development.

International Trade

Lardy (1994) has described the reemergence of China as a significant trading nation.[12] By 1993, China's total trade accounted for 2.5 percent of world trade, up from 0.8 percent in 1978. This means that China was the world's tenth largest exporter. It has also become a large debtor in the international capital market. Lardy explains that the commodity composition of trade has changed along with domestic market reforms, and that trade patterns (especially on the export side) are more consistent with China's comparative advantage, compared with the pre-reform and early reform time periods. China has shifted away from petroleum exports and has increased exports of labor-intensive manufactured goods, to the point where manufactured goods accounted for four-fifths of exports in 1993. Lardy notes that the share of primary commodities in total imports fell from a little over one-third in 1980 to about one-seventh by 1993, because food imports did not grow very much over this period while total imports surged.

China had been a net grain exporter during the 1950s. However, the sharp decline in grain production during the Great Leap Forward (1958–61) turned her into a net grain importer, with net imports averaging 3.45 mmt between 1961 and 1978. Grain imports were purposely increased during the first stage of reform (1978–84), to reduce farmers' procurement burden, to provide better incentives, and to encourage diversification in the agricultural sector (Carter and Zhong 1991a). The annual net imports averaged 12.46 mmt during the 1979–83 period. After 1984, following large increases in production and exports, combined with reduced on-farm wastage, annual net grain imports declined to 4.5 mmt between 1984 and 1991. The growth of corn production in northeast China contributed most to the increased grain exports. China exported 7.5 mmt of corn in 1991 and more than 10 mmt in 1992 and 1993, and this turned China into a net grain exporter in the early 1990s. However, when the central government suddenly banned rice and corn exports in late 1994, China resumed its position in world trade as a net grain importer.

Wheat has been the major grain imported by China since 1961, accounting for about 90 percent of total grain imports, on average. Canada, the United

---

12 In addition to Lardy (1994), refer to West (1993) for an in-depth discussion of China's trade reforms and trends in China's international trade patterns.

States, Australia, and Argentina are major suppliers of China's wheat imports. More recently, however, France and Great Britain have entered the market, with their combined share exceeding that of Australia and Argentina in 1990–91. The dominant position of wheat in grain imports may be challenged by feed grains, as more and more meat and dairy products will be demanded by consumers following income growth.

China was both a large rice exporter and importer in the last decade. Average annual exports during 1980–91 were 743,000 metric tons (mt), while average imports were 309,000 mt. Net annual exports were around 434,000 mt, on average. As the total world trade in rice was around 12 mmt per year during this time period, China's shares were about 6 and 4 percent, respectively, for total and net exports.

Southern China is suitable for growing Indica varieties of rice, and consumers in this region are accustomed to consuming these varieties. The current deficit position, and the likely further decline in grain production in this fast-developing region, may lead to a larger demand for imported Indica varieties of rice, both from central China and from abroad, for instance, from Thailand and Vietnam. On the other hand, Japan has partly opened its rice market, and China's northern provinces may view this as an opportunity to export Japonica varieties to Japan. However, there will be a partial offset through rising demand for Japonica by North China residents. Soybeans have also been a major grain export from China, averaging about 1 mmt until the 1994 export blockade.

For many countries, during the process of economic growth the nation's comparative advantage in agriculture declines, and this is expected to happen in China. For those nations where arable land is scarce, the comparative advantage in agriculture tends to decline more rapidly (Anderson and Hayami 1986; Anderson 1990). Generally speaking, the comparative advantage of China's agricultural sector has been declining for land-intensive crops. It is likely that China's net grain imports will increase in the future, with the composition gradually changing. In the long run, some shifting in imports from food to feed grains seems inevitable.

In 1994, the central government placed a (temporary) moratorium on grain exports in an effort to control higher domestic food prices. Given their importance in the urban consumers budget, food prices are an important contributor to the overall inflation rate.[13] Urban residents spent 50 percent of their incomes on food, and rural residents spent 58 percent, on average, in 1993. The

---

13 In 1994, the official inflation rate was around 20 percent per annum, but economists in China suggested it was probably several points higher in reality. Inflation in the mid-1990s was being fueled by rapid money-supply growth (over 30 percent per year), caused by a surge in foreign-exchange reserves and loose credit extension to state-owned enterprises.

blockade on exports is indicative of the fact that China's regional grain markets are not well integrated, and thus the central government is attempting to force provincial governments to sell on the domestic market rather than export. The workings of the domestic grain markets are discussed in more detail in Chapter 4.

Summary

China's economic reform began in agriculture, the success of which led to further reforms in other sectors of the economy. The absence of both product and input markets was a major factor responsible for inefficient resource allocation and low production incentives prior to reform. The basic objective of the economic reforms was to speed economic growth through improved incentives. In the agricultural sector, the reforms aimed to ensure greater supplies of grain and other important products through an improved decision-making process, including the introduction of (crude) market mechanisms.

Initially, the 1978 reforms in agriculture raised prices and gave farmers greater freedom to make production decisions (i.e., the household responsibility system: HRS). This led to substantial income growth for farmers. In addition, rural township and village enterprises (TVEs) were encouraged to develop and expand. The growth of TVEs has been the biggest success story in post-reform China. The TVEs absorbed labor that exited from agriculture.

Unfortunately, agriculture is now being left behind in the reform process. Farm incomes are falling well behind urban incomes. The initial effects of the HRS have petered-out and the government has moved backward with policy reform in agriculture. For instance, beginning in early 1994, the central government reestablished control of grain purchases and once again set fixed procurement prices. Farmers were once again forced to set planned acreage, because the central government operates under the belief that it must guarantee grain to major deficit cities and industrial areas, which means prices are not allowed to work effectively to send signals to surplus and deficit regions. There continues to be a major conflict between urban and rural residents over the price of grain. The poor incentives offered to farmers contributed to regional grain shortages in 1993, and interprovincial blockades took place on grain shipments out of surplus areas. In 1994, the situation with cotton was more serious, as up to one-third of the textile industry was without cotton.

Each provincial governor is now responsible for the provincial grain supply. Although this policy is especially designed to prevent further decline of grain-sown areas in the coastal provinces, it may temporarily improve grain supply in the coastal provinces at the cost of efficiency in resource allocation, and may encourage interprovincial blockades on grain shipment when some particular area suffers from a natural disaster. Farmers in coastal provinces may not take advantage of economic gains from further shifting of resources into more profitable activities, and those in inland grain-surplus regions may face relatively low prices for grain shipped to coastal provinces. In the long run, as past experience has shown, limiting the role of the market can only retard growth in the agricultural sector.

CHAPTER 3

The Slowdown of Agricultural Output Growth

As discussed in the previous chapter, when 1979–85 is compared with 1985–93, it is evident that the latter period experienced a slowdown in agricultural output growth. Some observers have noted that 1984 was an exceptionally good year for grains, having a bumper harvest, and that the downturn in yields in the latter half of the 1980s was not particularly unusual and was not an ominous sign that China had a major grain problem (Johnson 1994; Perkins 1992). However, others believe China is facing an agricultural crisis, primarily in grains (Aubert 1990; Guo 1988).

This chapter analyzes the question of whether or not there was a structural change in China's agricultural productivity growth in grain production after 1985. The analysis is restricted to grains because the household responsibility system (HRS) had a more profound impact on grains than on animal husbandry (Lin 1995). In addition, an examination of grains is appropriate given the government's preoccupation with self-sufficiency in grain production.

County-level data (from over 300 counties and over six years–1980, 1985, and 1987–90) were utilized to examine the question of what caused the slowdown in the growth of grain output in the late 1980s (see Carter and Zhang 1995, for full details of the analysis). Results indicate the slowdown was not due to a decline in the growth of input use, contrary to some common beliefs (for instance, see Yao 1994, p. 81). Instead, there was actually a loss in productivity in the 1985–92 time period, and this can be attributed to:

- Closing price-scissors (i.e., input prices rose faster than output prices);
- Diminishing returns from chemical fertilizer use;

- Limited opportunity to expand farm size; and
- Reduced government investment in agriculture.

Alternative Explanations for the Slowdown

There are two competing explanations for the decline in production growth after 1985 (Watson 1994). The "one-off privatization" school believes the 1978 reforms induced one-time productivity gains from privatization of farming and the subsequent slowdown in growth was to be expected. This explanation stresses the large contribution which the HRS made to the successful growth in China's agricultural productivity (Dong and Dow 1993; Fan 1991; Lin 1992; McMillan, Whalley, and Zhu 1989; Wen 1993). The HRS resulted in one-time productivity gains, and thus subsequent agricultural growth depended on technical change, which was not forthcoming.

Alternatively, the "market reform" school asserts that marketing reforms and price increases were relatively more important than privatization of farms, and it attributes the slowdown to stagnant prices and a reassertion of government controls over marketing. This school of thought emphasizes the relative importance of marketing reforms and price signals. These signals were positive in the early reform period but then became negative after 1984, when the government failed in its efforts to liberalize the grain markets and reinstated mandatory procurement controls (Sicular 1992). Our view is that the slowdown was due to return to more normal weather conditions in the late 1980s and to a loss in production efficiency after 1985, which appears to support the "market reform" explanation.

The grain-production increase in the early years of the reform period was mainly due to increased yields (see Table 2, Chap. 2), as the sown area to grain decreased from 120.6 million hectares (m. ha) in 1978 to 110.6 m. ha in 1992, a decline of 0.67 m. ha per year. There are two primary reasons for the fall in grain-sown area. First, farmers switched from grain production to more profitable cash crops. Second, rapid development of rural township and village enterprises displaced farmland that had previously been used for grain production.

In the first period of reform, the government grain policies focused on transforming the old communal farming system into the HRS and raising procurement prices for farm products, whereas the policies in the second period were geared more to reforming the marketing system. Attempts were made to establish a voluntary contract system to eliminate fixed procurement quotas and to reduce the central government's role in the grain market. These policies have largely failed, however (Economic Intelligence Unit 1994).

Analysis of County-Level Production

Carter and Zhang (1995) utilized disaggregated county-level data on grain production and five inputs: area sown to grain, labor, farm machinery, irrigation, and fertilizer.[1] In addition, they collected weather data, including monthly mean temperatures and total precipitation for each county. Weather and production data from 300 counties over six years (1980, 1985, and 1987–90) were used to estimate an aggregate grain-production model. This model provides estimates of grain-production elasticities for the inputs and the weather index, which in turn were used for growth accounting. *A Comprehensive Agricultural Regionalization of China*, published by the National Committee for Agricultural Regionalization of China (NCAR, 1984), was used for the division of grain-production regions in China. Based on the NCAR publication, the 300 sampled counties in this study were divided into five grain-producing regions: Northeast China, Huang-Huai-Hai River Basin (HHH), Middle and Lower Yangtze River Basin (MLY), Southwest China, and South China.

Growth accounting was conducted for the five grain-producing regions and for the two subperiods of 1978–84 and 1985–92; the results are presented in Table 3. Four points merit discussion. First, the higher output growth in the first period was attained with lower input growth compared to the second period. The average growth rate in aggregate inputs during the first period was 1.4 percent, compared with 2.3 percent in the second period. The lower growth rate in input usage in the first period was due largely to a decrease in sown area to grain and a decline in the mechanization level (Table 3). These results suggest that the slower growth in grain production in the second period (1985–92) was not due to a decline in the growth of input use.[2]

Second, weather plays an important role in determining grain production, and the effects of weather were quite different in the two periods. Good weather was found to contribute about 1.3 percent to the growth rate in grain production in the first period (1978–84). However, it contributed only 0.3 percent in the second period (1985–92). This suggests that about 1 percent of the decrease in the growth rate of grain production in the second period was due to more normal weather. Good or bad weather conditions should also be reflected

---

1 Note that there were no specific data for labor (N) and fertilizer (F) used in grain production at county level. These data were derived by multiplying the county's total agricultural labor (fertilizer) usage by the ratio of grain-sown area to total sown area, at the county level. This may introduce a bias, but it is a common approximation used in studying China's agriculture (Lin 1992).

2 However, it is worthwhile to note that the growth rate in chemical fertilizer use in the first period was 9.7 percent, compared with 7.8 percent in the second period. The slower growth rate in the latter period was due to runaway prices for chemical fertilizers and changes in fertilizer distribution policies (Ye and Rozelle 1994).

Table 3. Regional Grain Production Efficiencies, 1978–1984 and 1985–1992 (percent)

	1978–84 Period						1985–92 Period					
Description	Northeast China	HHH River Basin	MLY River Basin	Southwest China	South China	Nation	Northeast China	HHH River Basin	MLY River Basin	Southwest China	South China	Nation
Avg. growth rate in grain production	5.4	4.6	6.1	4.0	3.0	4.5	6.9	1.8	0.7	3.1	2.4	2.2
Growth rate in aggregate inputs	1.1	1.7	1.3	1.1	0.6	1.4	3.2	1.7	2.0	2.9	2.5	2.3
Of which:												
Labor	−0.8	0.3	−0.4	0.6	1.0	0.1	0.5	0.3	0.6	0.4	0.6	0.6
Sown area to grain	−0.1	−1.6	−0.3	−1.5	−2.5	−1.1	0.6	0.0	−0.3	0.9	0.1	0.2
Chemical fertilizer use	8.1	12.0	8.0	9.8	9.9	9.7	8.0	6.7	7.6	9.5	9.8	7.8
Percent of machine-ploughed area	−2.1	−4.7	−6.2	−7.0	−4.2	−3.9	4.9	6.2	10.3	9.9	4.9	7.0
Percent of irrigated area	−1.5	0.4	0.8	−0.7	−1.1	0.0	7.5	0.7	1.0	1.5	1.4	1.5
Weather's effects	1.1	1.4	1.8	0.9	0.8	1.3	0.5	0.1	0.2	0.7	0.8	0.3
Efficiency gains	3.2	1.5	3.0	2.0	1.6	1.8	3.1	0.0	−1.6	−0.6	−0.9	−0.4

Notes:
(1) The growth rate in aggregate input is a weighted average growth rate of all inputs. The weights are 0.235 for labor, 0.437 for sown area, 0.201 for fertilizer, 0.034 for machines, and 0.140 for irrigation.
(2) Provinces comprising individual regions: Northeast China includes Heilongjiang, Liaoning, and Jilin; HHH River Basin includes Shangdong, Hebei, Henan, Shanxi, and Nei Monggol; MLY River Basin includes Zhejiang, Jiangsu, Anhui, Hubei, Hunan, and Jiangxi; Southwest China includes Shanxi, Gansu, Sichuan, and Quizhou; South China includes Guangdong, Guangxi, Fujian, and Yunnan.
Source: Carter and Zhang (1995).

in the level of disaster-affected crop-sown area in China. According to official statistics, one hectare of disaster-affected crop means the yield in that area is 30 to 40 percent lower than the normal yield. The *Statistical Yearbook of China* (State Statistical Bureau [SSB], 1993) reported the average level of disaster-affected area to be about 17 m. ha annually in the first period (1978–84), but it was over 23 m. ha in the second period (1985–92).

Third, netting the growth rate in aggregate inputs and the effects of weather out of total production growth, the residual is the growth in total factor productivity (TFP). The growth in TFP, in this case, is due either to advances in technology or to increases in production efficiency (which includes both allocative and technical efficiencies).[3] Technological advance was not significant according to our regression analysis, which is perfectly plausible, as farming techniques and farm size have remained largely unchanged in China over the time period studied. Therefore, the growth in TFP in this context is reasoned to be due primarily to gains in production efficiency. In the first period (1978–84), the gains in production efficiency were estimated to be 3.3 percent, when the effects of weather were not removed. This suggests that the increases in production efficiency contributed about 70 percent (3.3/4.5) to the total growth in grain production, which is very close to the results reported by Lin (1992) and by McMillan, Whalley, and Zhu (1989) for approximately the same time period. However, when the effects of weather are taken out, the increase in production efficiency contributed about 40 percent (1.8/4.5) to the total growth in grain production, which is lower than the findings of Lin (1992) and others but which is closer to Carter and Zhong (1991a). For the second period (1985–92), the gains in production efficiency were between –0.4 and –0.1, with and without the effects of weather removed, respectively. The negative values suggest that there was a loss in efficiency in China's grain production in the second period.

Finally, there are considerable differences in the estimated gains in production efficiency across regions. In the first period, the Northeast achieved the highest efficiency gains in production (3.2 percent), followed by MLY River Basin (3 percent), Southwest (2 percent), and South China (1.6 percent). The HHH River Basin had the lowest gains (1.5 percent). In the second period, the Northeast almost attained the previous period's level in efficiency gains, but all other regions either had zero gains or suffered a loss in efficiency.

---

3 Note that this method of estimating production efficiency is a stylized application of Solow's (1957) residual measure of a country or region's movement toward or away from the production surface (i.e., the residual is equated with agricultural production efficiency). This is the same approach used by Johnson (1988).

What Led to the Productivity Slowdown?

The above analysis suggests that the slowdown in the growth rate in grain production in the post-HRS period (1985–92) was due to more normal weather conditions and to a loss in production efficiency during that period. Leaving explanations for weather patterns aside, four explanations are offered in the following paragraphs for the loss in production efficiency.

First, there was little or no technical progress in the post-HRS period (1985–92); available technology may have reached its limits, as grain yields are relatively high in China, compared to world standards.[4] At the beginning of the reforms, farmers were given the rights to cultivate and sell whatever crops they preferred as long as they fulfilled their contracts (e.g., for grain, cotton, or vegetables) set by the government. Farmers had strong incentives to work harder. As a result, both labor and land productivity increased rapidly. However, given the constraints of land and other farm facilities, the scale of household production may have quickly reached its efficiency frontier. Fertilizer has been the single most important factor in the growth of grain production in China, and the marginal gains from additional chemical fertilizer use may have tapered off.[5] The growth in fertilizer use contributed about 35 percent to the total growth in grain production during the period 1978–92. However, our sample of 300 counties shows that, on average, the marginal product of fertilizer in grain production decreased from 6.7 million tons of grain per 1,000 tons of fertilizer in 1980 to 3.8 million tons of grain per 1,000 tons of fertilizer in 1990.

Second, the profitability of farms in the second period was low compared with the first period. In the first period, the government raised procurement prices for farm products several times to encourage farmers to engage in agricultural production. McMillan, Whalley, and Zhu (1989) found that the effects of price increases accounted for about 22 percent of the total growth in China's agricultural production between 1978 and 1984. In the second period (1985–92), the government abolished quota prices and premiums and replaced them

---

4 See Crook (1993) for a discussion of problems encountered when interpreting official grain yields in China. China's State Land Administration has officially announced that China has about 120 million hectares of farmland, not just 100 million hectares, as long reported. Thus, potential arable land has been underreported by a factor of approximately 20 percent. Land taxes were originally based on land area and, over time, as new land was gradually brought into production, farmers did not necessarily have it added to the tax rolls. The revisions indicate that underreporting of actual cropped land has been about 14 percent, so yields have been overreported. The underreported land is not evenly distributed across regions and crops; it is believed that the underreporting is greatest in the northern part of the country.

5 However, a more balanced NPK (nitrogen, phosphorus, potassium) application ratio could improve productivity (Stone 1993, p. 346).

with a fixed contract price, which equaled the sum of quota prices and premiums, weighted by 0.7 and 0.3, respectively. The effective contract prices were actually lower than the previous prices. Since then, grain prices have failed to increase as rapidly as prices for farm inputs, such as fertilizer and pesticides. In addition, in the late 1980s, the government was short of funds to purchase contracted grain from farmers. Farmers were paid with IOUs, which led to peasant revolts in several provinces, such as Sichuan, Heilongjiang, and Anhui. The closing gap between farm-product prices and input prices, coupled with higher general inflation and higher taxes, seriously dampened farmers' incentives to grow grain.

Third, there has been a limited ability to introduce further mechanization and lower average costs through increasing farm size, because farms are so small. The average farm size is 0.5 ha (about 1.2 acres), with two to three family workers.[6] In the past few years, in some coastal areas, farmers have begun to form production and marketing cooperatives and have experimented with consolidating land holdings into partnerships to attempt to benefit from economies of scale. Our results indicate that the efficiency gains in production in the two northern regions (Northeast and HHH River Basin) are generally higher than in the three southern regions (MLY River Basin, Southwest, and South China). This is particularly obvious in the second period (1985–92). We believe this is partly due to higher economies of size in the northern regions. The ratio of grain-sown area to labor in the Northeast and the HHH River Basin is 0.9 ha and 0.23 ha, respectively; in comparison, it is only 0.16 ha in the MLY River Basin, 0.15 ha in the Southwest, and 0.12 ha in South China.

China is a country with scarce arable land per capita, which is particularly important because of its extremely large population. In 1992, the global average amount of arable land was 0.25 ha per capita, whereas the per capita arable land in China was only 0.08 ha. Throughout the 1980s, China's land area under cultivation had been decreasing, and the arable land per capita had fallen. Over the period 1978–93, the arable land per capita in China decreased at a rate of about 1.5 percent each year (from 0.1 hectares in 1978 to 0.08 in 1993).

There is some reason to believe that the expansion of farm size in China might lead to lower average costs of production. For instance, Rosner (1994) found that "economies of scale emerged in Taiwanese agriculture during the period of rapid industrialization" (p. 215). In addition, Kawagoe, Hayami, and Ruttan (1985) reported that agricultural production functions in developed nations are characterized by increasing returns to scale. Rosner (1994) reviewed

---

6 These small farms are not unique to East Asia, as over two-thirds of all farms in Japan, South Korea, and Taiwan operate on less than 1 ha (Rosner 1994). However, farms in these three countries are highly subsidized and, in addition, off-farm income is significant in Taiwan and Japan.

the farm size–productivity debate in East Asia, and he determined that Japanese data provide the strongest evidence that average costs decline as farm size increases. The evidence is less clear for South Korea and Taiwan. Rosner explained, "Industrialization and rising wage rates might not in themselves reduce the relative productivity of small farms, if farmers with a limited amount of land selected non-land intensive activities, or if markets for machine services were well developed and appropriate technology for small farms was available" (p. 24).

An unpublished report by the Jiangsu Rural Development Research Center (1994) describes an experiment on farm size that has been carried out in southern Jiangsu Province for the past several years. The sample covers thirty-three villages in three counties–Wuxi, Changshu, and Wuxian–where an average family farm is typically 0.15 to 0.26 ha, with each laborer working on less than 0.1 hectare. Because rural workers and their families cannot make a decent living on such a small farm, the experiment represents an attempt to establish an appropriate farm size–that is, a size adequate enough to provide farm workers with an income equivalent to that of workers in TVEs but not so large as to require a substantial amount of hired labor. The findings of the experiment are that, using existing techniques, one to two hectares per worker could meet the above criteria in southern Jiangsu Province. The enlargement in farm size may require an additional investment of 15,000 yuan per ha in infrastructure and machinery. Based on the findings of the experiment, if the village makes such an investment, farmers would be able to pay for the services received and still enjoy an adequate net income.

Because of China's excess rural labor force, agriculture cannot enjoy economies of scale by expanding farm size. In other countries with rich land resources, capital has been substituted for labor as part of the process of economic growth, resulting in large-scale farms with high labor productivity. These countries, namely the United States, Canada and Australia, have become major producers and exporters of farm products in the world. In China, owing to the labor surplus, it is not rational to substitute capital for labor. Thus, expanding farm size is not an effective way to raise returns to factors of production in China's agriculture (Cai 1990). The motivation for and result of maintaining small-scale farming have accelerated the decline of comparative advantage in agriculture, especially the comparative advantage in grain production, which uses more arable land but less labor.

Finally, government investment in agriculture has decreased. Table 4 shows that between 1976 and 1980, agriculture's share in total government construction spending averaged 10.5 percent. This share started to decline after 1981 but remained above 5 percent until 1985. However, beginning in 1985, the share decreased, ranging between 3 and 4 percent from 1985 to 1993. Not only

Table 4. Government and State Enterprise Construction Investment, 1976–1993

Year	Total investment (bil. yuan)	Investment in agriculture (bil. yuan)	Total share of agriculture (%)
1976–80	234.2	24.61	10.5
1981	44.29	2.92	6.6
1982	55.55	3.41	6.1
1983	59.41	3.55	5.9
1984	74.32	3.71	5.0
1985	107.44	3.59	3.3
1986	117.61	3.51	3.0
1987	134.31	4.21	3.1
1988	157.43	4.75	3.0
1989	155.07	5.07	3.2
1990	170.38	6.72	3.9
1991	211.58	8.50	4.0
1992	301.27	11.27	3.7
1993	461.55	n.a.	n.a.

Source: *Statistical Yearbook of China* (SSB, 1993, Tables 5-5 and 5-18).

has the share of agriculture in total government investment declined, the absolute value in some years was lower in the second period (1985–92) than in the first period (1978–84). For example, total government investment in agriculture was about 3.5 billion yuan in 1985 and 1986, which was lower than the 4.9 billion yuan yearly average, between 1976 and 1980 (in nominal terms). After adjusting the figures for inflation, the decline was about 50 percent. The consequence of lower government investment and very little private investment is that rural infrastructure, such as roads and irrigation canals, is not well maintained and is deteriorating. Private investment is minimal because there is no private ownership of farmland. Most farmers in the early 1980s signed fifteen-year leases with the township or village, and such a short lease period provides little incentive to make long-term improvements to the land base. As of September 1994, land leases have been extended to thirty years (see Prosterman, Hanstad, and Ping 1994, p. 21).

Summary

The productivity gains associated with the 1978 introduction of China's household responsibility system are well documented in several studies. However, less is known about the subsequent slowdown of agricultural output in the mid-1980s. This chapter has attempted to explain the slowdown in grain output growth from 1985 to 1992. There are two schools of thought explaining the decline in growth after 1985. The "one-off privatization" school believes the 1978 reforms induced one-time productivity gains from the privatization of farming and thus the slowdown in the late 1980s was to be expected. The second market reform school believes that other marketing reforms, such as price increases and a reduction in mandatory procurement, were relatively more important than privatization of farming, and it attributes the slowdown to stagnant prices and a reassertion of government marketing controls in the 1980s.

Our results suggest that the slowdown after 1985 was due to more normal weather conditions and failure in government policies to liberalize markets. Attempts to reform China's grain marketing system failed and farmers became discouraged by low profitability. The wage gap between the urban and rural households led to an exodus of skilled labor from agriculture and the government budget deficit resulted in a decline in public investment in it. Meanwhile, uncertainty over land tenure resulted in less private investment. As a result, grain output growth stagnated.

CHAPTER 4

The Role of Markets

Prior to reform, all farm products were classified into three categories by the government. The goods in the first category, including grain, edible oil and oil-bearing crops, and cotton, were subject to so-called *tong gou*, or unified procurement. The government was the sole buyer of goods in this category, through the compulsory quota system. Basic quotas were fixed for a three- to five-year period, along with production targets, and farm products were procured at fixed prices. The quantities of above-quota deliveries were also compulsory and were set as a certain percentage of the production exceeding the target levels. These goods were usually purchased at a 20 to 30 percent premium above the quota price. The goods could not be sold on the free market, and the surplus (if producers were willing) could be sold to the government at a "negotiated price," also unilaterally set by the government.

The goods in the second category were subject to *pai gou*, or imposed purchases, and consisted of meat and aquatic products, tobacco, tea, silk, and sugar crops. The government set compulsory procurement quotas and corresponding prices for these products, but permitted sales on the free market after producers fulfilled their delivery obligations.

There were no compulsory quotas for the goods in the third category, which consisted mainly of vegetables and fruits, and some industrial crops. However, because long-distance trading was not permitted for producers, government agencies had dominant power in marketing these goods, especially the industrial crops, and hence were able to set prices to a large extent.

Policy reform also affected the "retail" and "wholesale" supply of grain and other industrial crops to urban and industrial consumers. In 1985, the subsidized supply of grain to processing and manufacturing enterprises was ended. From 1985, those enterprises had either to pay the "negotiated price," or to buy directly from the free market. Urban retail prices for rationed goods to consumers were increased substantially in 1991 and 1992. At the same time, urban residents were turning to the free markets, in search of better-quality food. Ultimately, the rationing of grain in the urban areas was abolished in most cities by 1993. However, in 1994, when the retail price of grain increased sharply, some cities restored low-price grain rationing for the urban poor in an effort to stabilize prices in the free market.

At present, free markets operate for the following goods: meat, aquatic products, edible oil, tea, silk, sugar, fruits, vegetables, some grains (potatoes, sorghum, barley, millet, peas, beans, and oats), and other industrial crops. However, rice, wheat, corn, sorghum, and cotton prices are still set at artificially low levels, and farmers must fulfill quota delivery obligations before selling any surplus grain onto the free markets. Cotton cannot be sold on the free market.

In addition to farm products, most of the farm inputs were also controlled by the state prior to reform. Exceptions on the input side were intermediate goods produced on the farm and farm tools produced at rural small workshops. Farmers were free to trade these with each other. Farm machinery was allocated through quota or plans, the supply was often short, and prices were subsidized. Other manufactured inputs, such as chemical fertilizer, pesticides, diesel fuel, and plastic sheeting, were provided through a quota system. This was also true of some seeds. The quotas were generally based on production and/or procurement plans, in order to facilitate policy goals. This section provides a discussion of the pace, depth, and success of reform of the above-mentioned markets, highlighting developments in farm product markets.[1]

Reform of Product Markets

The 1978 reforms legalized existing free markets and permitted private trade in some controlled products, such as grain, provided that the procurement quota had first been filled. Following the adoption of the HRS and the associated boost in agricultural production, free markets quickly developed in terms of an increased number of county fairs, and increased volumes traded. For most products, long-distance private trading was gradually allowed, leading to the emergence of regional and even national markets.

The development of regional and national markets was complementary to efforts to commercialize the agricultural sector. The 1978 reform permitted

1 See Sicular (1988, 1993, 1995) and Rozelle (1994) for additional discussion of the development of marketing channels for China's agricultural products.

Table 5. Free Markets in Urban and Rural Areas

Description	1980	1984	1985	1986	1987	1988	1989	1990	1991	1992	1993
Number of markets:	40,809	56,500	61,337	67,610	69,683	71,359	72,130	72,579	74,675	79,188	83,001
Urban	2,919	6,144	8,013	9,710	10,908	12,181	13,111	13,106	13,891	14,510	16,450
Rural	37,890	50,356	53,324	57,909	58,775	59,178	59,019	59,473	60,784	64,678	66,551
Value of transactions (bil. yuan):	23.54	45.69	63.32	90.65	115.70	162.13	197.36	216.82	262.22	353.00	534.30
Urban	2.37	7.52	12.0	24.44	34.17	54.53	72.36	83.78	107.92	158.30	526.24
Rural	21.17	38.17	51.16	66.21	81.08	107.60	125.00	133.04	154.29	194.70	278.06
Of which:											
Grain and edible oil	3.44	4.56	4.96	7.12	8.47	10.81	14.27	14.68	16.47	21.30	34.99
Meat, fowl, and eggs	4.21	9.18	14.01	24.68	32.03	46.00	57.06	61.88	70.55	85.91	110.25
Aquatic products	0.93	2.41	3.32	6.44	8.54	12.30	15.80	18.24	22.42	29.22	41.36
Vegetables	2.15	3.83	4.88	9.69	13.11	19.30	23.82	26.42	33.19	43.46	58.20
Dried and fresh fruits	0.75	1.86	2.55	5.93	8.31	12.29	16.10	18.35	23.34	29.13	40.32
Agricultural inputs	0.71	1.31	1.39	1.52	1.58	1.83	2.22	2.30	2.45	2.95	n.a.
Large domestic animals	2.65	3.56	3.26	3.11	3.26	3.82	3.89	3.83	4.36	4.79	5.67

Source: *Statistical Yearbook of China* (SSB, various years).

some diversification in the farming sector, and decentralization of the decision-making process stimulated farmers to shift their focus to specialized and commercialized production. This resource reallocation led to significant structural changes in the agricultural sector. In real terms, the fishery subsector increased almost four times from 1978 to 1994, and animal husbandry doubled in size, while the cropping sector increased by 55 percent during the same time period. In 1978, cropping accounted for 80 percent of the gross value of agricultural output (GVAO), but this share declined to 58 percent by 1994. This was more in line with the sector's comparative advantage, and within the cropping sector there was some shift toward more labor-intensive crops. As a result, the production of products available for county fair sales increased dramatically.

As the government gradually reduced the number of items subject to compulsory procurement, as well as the government's role in supplying agricultural products at subsidized prices, free markets continued to expand. It was reported that, by the end of 1992, about 70 percent of the total sales of agricultural products took place at market prices (International Monetary Fund 1993). The total number of "free markets" in urban and rural areas doubled from 40 thousand in 1980 to 83 thousand by 1993 (see Table 5), and the value of trade in these markets increased from 23.54 to 534 billion yuan.

Encouraged by the success of the increased agricultural production, and facing a larger volume of trade in agricultural commodities, the government took measures to loosen restrictions on interregional private trade and established several trading centers for farm products, such as the Zhengzhou Grain Market and the Shanghai Grain and Edible Oil Exchange.

By late 1993, only corn, wheat, rice, soybeans, cotton, and tobacco were still subject to some type of government control. In the case of grain, a new procurement policy was announced: *bao liang fang jia*, or "fixing the quantity while freeing the price." Under the 1993 policy, the so-called contracted purchasing quota, which had replaced the *tong gou* as a new form of compulsory procurement in 1985, remained in effect, but the price was to be at the "market" level instead of fixed in advance. On the retail side, urban residents were still entitled to obtain a rationed quantity but had to pay the market price. In other words, the government purchasing and marketing agencies would remain in business, but mostly on a commercial basis, competing with private and collective enterprises.

By the end of 1993, however, this policy proved to be unsuccessful. In December 1993, the central government placed a ceiling on grain retail prices in order to prevent any possible social unrest associated with the fast growth in food prices in urban areas, and the procurement price was fixed again for the next year. Once again, mandatory procurement proved to be at the core of China's grain policy.

Beginning in early 1994, the central government reestablished control of grain purchases and once again set fixed procurement prices. And again, farmers were forced to set planned acreage because the central government operates under the belief that it must guarantee grain to major deficit cities and industrial areas, which means prices are not allowed to work effectively to send signals to surplus and deficit regions. There continues to be a major conflict between urban and rural residents over the price of grain. The poor incentives offered to farmers contributed to regional grain shortages in 1993, and interprovincial blockades took place on grain shipments out of surplus areas. In 1994, the situation with cotton was more serious, as up to one-third of the textile industry was without it. The textile plants were unable to start operations, and textile workers went without jobs. Cotton production was 6 mmt in 1985, but fell to 3.7 mmt for 1994, largely due to poor economic signals originating with the central government, and a bollworm infestation in the early 1990s (Colby 1993).

In his government report to the Peoples Congress on March 5, 1995, Premier Li Peng called for each provincial governor to be responsible for *mi daiz* (rice bag), that is, responsible for the provincial grain supply. In his words, this requires provincial governors "to ensure sown areas, improve yields, increase reserves, coordinate supply with demand, and stabilize prices." In reality, it implies strengthening and enforcing the sown-area plan and procurement quota, especially designed to prevent further decline of grain-sown areas in the coastal provinces. This policy may temporarily improve grain supply in the coastal provinces at the cost of efficiency in resource allocation, and may encourage interprovincial blockades on grain shipment when a particular area suffers from a natural disaster. Farmers in coastal provinces may not take advantage of economic gains from further shifting of resources into more profitable activities, and those in inland grain-surplus regions may face relatively low prices for grain shipped to coastal provinces. In the long run, as past experience shows, limiting the role of the market can only slow growth in the agricultural sector.

From the mid-1980s, control of cotton marketing has been even more restrictive than that of grain. Procurement is more rigorously enforced for cotton and there is no free market. Because the textile industry provides significant profit and tax revenue at the low cotton price, political conflicts are often reported between farmers and government, and between different levels of government. The central government tries to enforce the planned distribution, the local governments in producing areas want to keep as much cotton as possible for the local mills, and manufacturers in other areas are willing to pay a higher price. While competing with each other, farmers reduce their production in response to the low price, hold inventories from delivery, and try to sell to manufacturers directly. The so-called cotton purchasing war became more

Table 6. Grain Procurement by the State, 1978–1993

Year	Grain production (mmt)	Quantity procured (mmt)	Percent procured (%)
1978	304.77	50.73	16.65
1979	332.12	60.10	18.10
1980	320.56	61.29	19.12
1981	325.02	68.46	21.06
1982	354.50	78.06	22.02
1983	387.28	102.49	26.46
1984	407.31	117.25	28.79
1985	379.11	107.63	28.39
1986	391.51	115.16	29.41
1987	402.98	120.92	30.01
1988	394.08	119.95	30.44
1989	407.55	121.38	29.78
1990	446.24	139.95	31.36
1991	435.29	136.36	31.32
1992	442.65	132.46	29.92
1993	456.48	n.a.	n.a.

Source: *Statistical Yearbook of China* (SSB, various years).

and more serious, recently as the gap between the procurement price and the market price widened. Although the central government puts greater pressure on the regional governments year after year, the cotton war continues, and presumably will persist as long as the market is tightly controlled.

Although reform in the agricultural marketing and pricing area has been quite substantial for some products, it still has a long way to go. The number of free markets, quantities, and items traded, numbers of farmers' marketing organizations, and so on, all have increased. Simultaneously, the number of products subject to fixed prices has continued to decline over the last fifteen years. However, the central government is still experiencing problems in lifting its controls over the marketing of grain and cotton. For example, an attempt at decontrol was made in 1991, when the central government introduced a grain reserve program that promoted food security and price stabilization objectives. However, the main mechanisms for managing and financing the reserve program were never clearly established, and thus it failed. Consequently, the central government continues to procure about one-third of all grain produced (see Table 6). Of the total amount procured, about 82 percent is purchased through either quota or negotiated channels.

Reform in the Input Markets

Besides intermediate goods produced on farm and tools produced as sideline products, the major agricultural inputs include land, labor, credit, and manufactured goods such as chemical fertilizer, pesticides, diesel fuel, and plastic sheeting. Markets for all of these inputs have been established, to some extent, during the reform period. While this subsection briefly discusses the development of input markets to date, later sections will discuss, in more detail, issues related to labor and financial markets as they have other important implications beyond the scope of this chapter.

Land

Established in the late 1950s, the Rural People's Commune was a compulsory and closed "cooperative." In most cases, land was owned by the production team and was nontransferable. When the HRS was introduced in the late 1970s, land-use rights were contracted out to individual farmers for a certain time period, but were still nontransferable. Initially, the length of the land lease was short, about three to five years; then it was extended to fifteen years in the mid-1980s, and to thirty years in 1993.

In addition, land-use rights were made inheritable and transferable in the early 1980s (within the length of the lease), in order to increase the sense of security for farmers and to encourage long-term investment. Farmers were allowed to claim monetary compensation for investments if land-use rights were transferred. The 1988 constitutional amendment formally legalized the transfer of land-use rights, but in practice it was very rare, as most farmers could not find off-farm jobs and had to rely on farming to make a living.

Labor

Prior to reform, farmers were prohibited from taking outside work without permission. Members were assigned a job with the commune or brigade enterprise, and often the wage was paid directly to the respective team, not to the worker. After the reform, many private enterprises emerged within the collectives (they are now called TVEs), and "hired" labor became inevitable. The government responded to the practical needs of the labor market, formally recognizing the right to hire and to be hired, and gradually loosened restrictions on the number of individuals employed in a single enterprise.

By the early 1990s, many TVEs in the coastal regions actually relied on workers from inland regions. Sometimes the workers were from thousands of kilometers away. Seasonal employment also became a common phenomenon in farming, as many farmers had moved to the urban areas or coastal regions to seek nonfarm jobs. In 1992, approximately 35.75 million farmers lived temporarily in cities and towns every day (on average), and the majority found jobs there (Ministry of Agriculture, Research Center for Rural Economy, 1993). The large number of transient workers contributed to the problems in the urban areas of rising unemployment and crime rates, as well as placing additional burdens on public utilities.

In order to maintain social stability, which, particularly in the urban areas, has always been a top government policy priority, the central government has been reluctant to free up the labor market. The local governments in urban areas are even more opposed to rural–urban labor migration and they have instituted a number of disincentives and penalties for employers who hire transient farmers. For instance, local governments have invoked special "public utility" levies against employers who hire transients. The new restrictions, together with the existing residence registration system and the nonexistence of a housing market, make labor migration very difficult.

If a unified social security system is established in the future, the unemployment and health insurance would become society's responsibility, and housing would be provided through the market, not by enterprises. In that case, the labor market would have a more solid ground on which to further develop. Otherwise, a free labor market cannot exist, regardless of what regulations are formally announced.

Other Inputs

A system of Rural Credit Cooperatives was established during the 1950s, and these were basically owned by farmers. However, these cooperatives evolved into semigovernmental bodies, with loans being allocated according to a central plan. These policy loans were usually in the form of advance payments for grain procurement, related to production and delivery of specified crops. The loans were often interest free.

This situation has not changed significantly, although the Rural Credit Cooperative and the Agricultural Bank are now more commercialized. Lacking collateral, most farmers have no access to these formal financial institutions. Moreover, administrative costs would likely be very high if these institutions were to begin dealing with farmers who operate on only one acre of land. Thus, the major service of the cooperatives to farmers still consists of allocating policy loans in the form of advance payments for grain or for cotton procurement.

As returns on loans to TVEs and other nonagricultural businesses are much higher than the policy-fixed interest rates, the cooperatives sometimes channel money for policy loans into other loans or investments. In this case, farmers are given a term-deposit certificate in lieu of the advance payment. On delivery, procured goods are paid for in full, the deposit and the loan are canceled out, and the interest on the term deposit is paid to the farmers. A large part of farmers' savings with the cooperatives is used to finance TVEs or is transferred into the urban areas.

Up to the mid-1980s, the distribution of major manufactured inputs was monopolized by the Agricultural Input Corporations at the wholesale level, and by the Supply and Marketing Cooperatives at the retail level. Originally, the Supply and Marketing Cooperatives were farmer owned, but in time they became state controlled and managed. Chemical fertilizer, diesel, and other modern inputs were allocated through the central-provincial-county planning channel, based on availability and the amount of acreage that was sown to specific crops.

This situation was unchanged after the urban enterprise reform commenced in the mid-1980s and the two-track price system was adopted to stimulate industrial production. Under the two-track price system, industrial enterprises were assigned production targets as before, with planned supplies of inputs at a "planned price." The above-target output could be sold to the government at a "negotiated price," or onto the market if permitted. Accordingly, inputs beyond the plan were bought at either negotiated or market prices. In this case, as the government was unwilling to incur further subsidies, manufactured inputs were supplied to farmers at both planned and negotiated prices. Usually the quantity of inputs supplied at planned prices was fixed in relation to sown area procurement quotas, as before, and farmers could buy additional supplies at either negotiated or market prices.

In 1993, the government announced its intention to further reform the farm input market, including abolishing the two-track price system. For manufactured inputs, the government proposed paying farmers a fixed amount of money to substitute for the price subsidy. Although this change might have positive effects on allocation efficiency, farmers complained that under the new strategy their support would actually be reduced, as the previous input price subsidy generally increased with market prices whereas the value of the newly proposed monetary compensation would be fixed in amount.

The 1993–1995 Food Price Increases

The rapid increase in retail food prices beginning in late 1993 generated considerable interest both inside and outside of China. Why did grain prices rise so rapidly? First, many observers wondered why grain prices rose so much when a large grain reserve was apparently established in the 1980s.[2] Crook (1993,1994b) compared the U.S. Department of Agriculture's (USDA's) stock estimates with those from sources in China. In 1990, published reports in China estimated 490 million metric tons (mmt) of grain stocks, while the USDA estimated stocks to be only 82 mmt. There are several possible explanations for the large discrepancy. China has published little information on the size of its grain reserve. Estimates based on limited information from the government may be confusing as China does not clearly distinguish seasonal storage from "reserve stocks" kept for security reasons. The government Grain Marketing Bureaus normally complete procurement in November or December, and they typically handle about 90 mmt of grain annually. Therefore, the year-end figure for grain storage is very high. Any estimates based on such figures could be misleading. Furthermore, many reports have revealed that the actual volumes of grain in state "reserves" are well below the official figures in many locations, and that its quality is not suitable for human consumption (Deng 1993).

Second, after three years of retrenchment (1988–91), China experienced another period of rapid economic growth in 1992, which led to double-digit inflation in 1993. For example, the prices of manufactured agricultural inputs increased by 14.1 percent, compared to an annual increase of 3 to 5 percent during the previous three years (1990–92). Prices of fuel and building materials increased by 32.2 percent and 28.2 percent, respectively, in the rural areas in 1993. These large increases in production costs helped push up food prices in 1993. The inflation rate was even higher in 1994, as the consumer retail price was reported to have increased by 21.8 percent in 1994, compared with 13.2 percent in 1993.[3]

Third, the remaining compulsory procurement system makes grain prices very sensitive to local supply and demand conditions. When the policy changed early in 1993 to one of grain procurement at "free market" prices, it disturbed the imperfect grain market. Partly as a consequence, food prices went up by 30 percent in one month in the coastal provinces in November 1993 (Lin 1994). Subsequently, the policy reversal and reintroduction of fixed procurement prices at the end of 1993 sent the wrong signals to farmers in surplus areas, discouraging them from increasing production the next year. The reintroduction of fixed procurement prices at the end of 1993 was partly responsible for the 2.8 percent decline in grain production in 1994. This occurred despite sharp increases in market prices.

The 1993 changes in the procurement and rationing policy deserve more detailed explanation. The overall objective of the policy remains one of extracting resources from the agricultural sector in order to finance industrializa-

---

2 For a discussion of grain stock estimates, see Crook (1988 and 1994b).
3 *Statistical Yearbook of China,* 1994 (Beijing: Statistical Publishing House, 1995).

tion through the price channel while simultaneously ensuring an adequate food supply. Because this policy has not worked very well, the procurement prices were doubled for most grain crops during the 1979–92 time period, to encourage farmers to expand grain production.

At the beginning of the 1978 economic reforms, the government did not raise grain retail prices in the urban areas, because that could only lead to wage increases in the urban areas where state employment is dominant. However, as the share of urban nongovernment sectors increased, and as the government established a form of contracted management for the state enterprises, the state announced an increase in the grain retail price in the urban areas for the purposes of reducing the budget burden associated with subsidizing grain resales. As the result, the retail price for rationed grain was increased by 20.7 percent in 1991, and another 39.2 percent in 1992, on average (Lin 1994).

The large increase in the rationing price closed the gap between the government and free-market prices to a large extent, and urban consumers shifted part of their daily purchases to the free markets where product quality was higher. Thus, the quantity of monthly rationing was no longer binding, and the pressure on the government to ensure a food supply was relaxed. Coupled with three years of bumper harvests (about 10 percent above the 1989 level), the government was confident enough to pursue further marketing reforms in 1993. Almost all provinces abolished the rationing of grain and edible oils by late 1993, and the fixed price for "contracted purchasing" also was abolished. Although farmers were still obliged to sell a fixed specified quantity (quota) of grain to the government, the price was to be at the "market" level.

However, the government did not specify which "market price" would be for procurement purposes. This uncertainty associated with the policy created problems in both deficit and surplus areas. In the Southeast coastal areas where grain supply is short, farmers and the local government found better production opportunities and shifted their resources to more profitable production activities. The area sown to grain crops declined by 10 percent in Zhejiang, 5 percent in Fujian, and 8 percent in Guangdong, and grain output declined in these provinces by 8, 5, and 10 percent, respectively. In the surplus areas, farmers withheld grain deliveries in the fall of 1993, anticipating higher prices. Local governments in these areas responded by prohibiting outward grain shipments, in order to enforce the "quota delivery first" policy, with the objective of reducing their procurement expenditures. The blockade, along with the market shortage, resulted in the big jump in grain retail prices in the southeast coastal areas, which soon spread over the whole country.

The central government was concerned about the sharp increase in grain retail prices in the urban areas, out of fear that it might threaten social stability and economic growth. So it placed a ceiling on retail prices and released 2.5

mmt of grain from reserve. Compulsory procurement was to be strictly enforced again. The signals received by farmers from the local and central governments discouraged grain production and contradicted the free-market signals, leading to a fall in grain production by 2.8 percent in 1994. By the middle of 1994, the central government had placed a ban on rice and corn exports, and later on, several provincial governments prohibited grain shipments to other provinces.

However, as the population continued to grow at 1.1 to 1.15 percent, and per capita real incomes continued to increase (by 7.8 and 5 percent, respectively, in the urban and rural areas in 1994),[4] the demand for food rose. The supply situation in urban areas became more severe as an increasing number of farmers sought jobs in the coastal areas. According to the *Chinese Business Times*,[5] food prices in the rural areas in November 1994 were 41.4 percent higher than in 1993, which suggests an even larger increase in the coastal urban areas.

The domestic vegetable, edible oil, and grain markets experienced massive price increases from 1994 to 1995. This was partly due to expectations of provincial authorities and increasingly protective practices by provincial government trading authorities reluctant to allow food products to leave their provincial boundaries. For example, for several months in 1995, Heilongjiang Province, in the far northeast, would not permit soybean shipments out of the province. The rising protectionism of the provinces is a serious problem.

Summary

Past experience clearly suggests that market-oriented reform is the key to faster growth in Chinese agriculture. However, this does not imply that the Chinese government will push rapid market reform. The policy response to the 1993–94 bout of inflation indicates that the government is quite willing to fall back on administrative measures in order to control prices and control the supply of basic goods like grain and cotton.

The major reason for the government's reluctance to reform the market further may be related to its long-term policy orientation: fast industrialization, which requires a supply of cheap food and other inputs, as well as political stabilization in the urban-industrial sector. Therefore, fundamental change in the grain and cotton market may not occur in the near future.

Government control of cotton marketing has been even more restrictive than it has been for grain. Procurement is more rigorously enforced for cotton and

---

4 *People's Daily*, December 31, 1994.
5 *Chinese Business Times*, December 29, 1994.

there is no free market. Because the textile industry provides significant profit and tax revenue at the low cotton price, political conflicts are often reported between farmers and government, and between different levels of government. The central government tries to enforce the planned distribution, the local governments in producing areas want to keep as much cotton as possible for the local mills, and manufacturers in other areas are willing to pay a higher price.

There are numerous remaining inefficiencies in China's marketing system (e.g., monopoly government agencies, grading, transportation, storage, market information, market failures, etc.). The lack of interregional trade is still a significant problem in China and acts as a drag on further economic growth. Lack of regional integration also contributes to the growing disparity of incomes between prosperous (coastal) and less prosperous (inland and western) regions.

Unlike reform in the product markets, further reform in the farm input market implies reducing budget subsidies and increasing state enterprise profits, both of which are consistent with the objective of speeding up industrialization. Because returns to agriculture are relatively low, further reform of financial markets may also divert financial resources out of agriculture. Therefore, the input and financial markets are likely to develop faster than the product, land, or labor markets.

CHAPTER 5

Excess Labor in Agriculture

China's rural population and number of agricultural workers are enormous: the total population is approaching 1.2 billion, and China's rural population accounts for roughly three-fourths of this number. Likewise, about three-fourths of the employed population is rural (but estimates of these ratios vary). The *Statistical Yearbook of China* 1994 (State Statistical Bureau), reports that approximately 350 million workers remain in China's agriculture, which represents about 80 percent of the rural work force (440 million in total). However, based on the recent 1990 National Population Census, the rural labor force is actually much larger: 480 million in total, and 421 million in agriculture (Population Census Office, 1993). What is surprising is that this very large discrepancy in the official labor statistics is not widely discussed, with the exception of Banister and Harbaugh (1992). The discrepancy is due to alternative definitions of labor-force ages, different sampling procedures, and timing of the sampling.

Because of imperfections in the labor market (i.e., largely due to the *hukou* system), many individuals have little choice but to stay on their family farm and share work with other family members. That the resulting rural underemployment is indeed a large problem in China appears to be generally acknowledged (Prosterman, Hanstad and Ping 1994; Taylor 1993; Yao 1994, p. 10), and there could be over 100 million surplus workers in the sector (Deng 1991; Annual Rural Analysis Group, 1994 p. 24). For instance, Jiang Liu (1994), China's Minister of Agriculture, has recently stated that "one-third of the 438 million rural workers is in surplus." This rather large number of estimated underemployed is supported by evidence published elsewhere. For example, in the

1995 issue of the *Economic Green Report* (Annual Rural Analysis Group 1995, p. 12), it was estimated that excess labor in the rural areas totals about 120 million. According to the 1994 *Economic Green Report* (Chap. 1), in Anhui Province about 50 percent of the current agricultural labor force is considered to be surplus labor. Taylor (1993) provides an exhaustive survey of academic articles in China on rural underemployment, and he finds evidence that 30–40 percent of China's rural workers are redundant. He believes estimates from within China of rural underemployment in the range of 100 million persons to be realistic. Taylor explains: "The primary reason why rural surplus labour has continued to exist in China is that tight restrictions on rural-to-urban migration and the existence of fixed land resources in rural areas have simply forced more peasants to make a living from tilling the soil than is necessary" (Taylor 1993, p. 282).

The notion that developing countries can be characterized as having "surplus" rural labor (or disguised unemployment) is attributed to Lewis (1954, 1958). Fei and Ranis (1964) found evidence in support of the idea that disguised unemployment exists, as have a number of other researchers (see Oshima 1958). However, the Lewis postulate is quite controversial; some economists argue that, theoretically, surplus labor cannot exist, and they have criticized the Lewis model for its implication that the marginal productivity of labor may be zero in agriculture (see Jorgenson 1970; Schultz 1964). The contention that such a problem could not even exist is presumably based on the (theoretical) belief that the labor market is fully functional, and thus workers leaving the farm could always find some type of work—which is not the case in China.

Lewis argued that it is irrelevant whether the marginal productivity of farm labor is zero or just less than the wage rate. Johnston (1970) suggests that Lewis has been misinterpreted by some scholars. He points out that Lewis did not subscribe to the naive view that a large percentage of the labor force could be removed from agriculture, leaving the level of agriculture output unchanged, without substituting some other inputs or additional labor from those remaining in farming. In fact, Lewis argued that workers who stayed in agriculture could maintain output by their willingness and ability to work harder. Similarly, Johnston and Mellor (1960) suggested that the remaining stock of labor would be utilized more intensively.

The empirical evidence is mixed on the question of whether or not farm labor is redundant in developing countries. For instance, Jorgenson (1970) draws on the earlier work of Oshima (1958), and notes that China did not have a problem of surplus labor in the 1950s: "The situation in south-eastern Europe, Egypt, China, and Southeast Asia appears to be one of labor shortage rather than labor surplus" (Jorgenson 1970, p. 340). Jorgenson also writes, "To date, there is little reliable empirical evidence to support the existence of more than token—5 percent—disguised unemployment in underdeveloped countries" (p. 342). Alternatively, Lin explains that, in China in the 1950s, "The main rationale for collectivization was rooted in the notion that mobilizing rural *surplus* labor would increase rural capital formation and, hence, increase production" (Lin 1995, p. 7; italics added). So it seems that China's officials were of the view in the 1950s, as they are now, that surplus farm labor is a problem. We are also of the opinion that there is a problem of surplus labor in China, and its existence can be explained by the fact that the labor market does not function properly due to restrictions on labor mobility.

This chapter provides an analysis of the extent of labor underemployment in agriculture. However, it is difficult to estimate the magnitude of this problem, partly due to data inconsistencies. The discrepancies between year-end population and labor-force statistics published in the State Statistical Bureau's *Statistical Yearbook of China* and those recorded in the Population Census Office's *National Population Census* data are discussed. We also briefly describe the imperfections in the labor market. Secondary data are used to examine the difference between available workdays in the rural population versus the number of days required to produce given levels of farm and other outputs. Subtracting the number of man-days required to maintain both agricultural and nonagricultural outputs at the current level from the number of man-days available gives a rough indication of the level of underemployment. This approach implicitly assumes that the workers remaining in agriculture work harder and that there is some (minimal) substitution of nonlabor inputs for the labor that exited.

Rural Population and the Agricultural Labor Force

The present distribution of the population and the labor force across urban and rural areas is the result of the long-running, industry-oriented development strategy. In the early 1950s, the communist government chose a strategy of giving top priority to the development of heavy industry. In order to implement this strategy in the capital-scarce economy, the government introduced a package of policies to reduce the production cost of heavy industry by distorting the prices of commodities and the basic factors of production.

Urban labor costs were reduced by a "cheap food" policy and urban housing subsidies. To maintain this urban-biased regime, the commune system tightly controlled farm-worker migration, thereby preventing rural workers from

Table 7. International Comparison of Employment in Agriculture

International economies	Per capita GNP ($U.S.)	Rural population (% of total)	Employment in agriculture (% of total)
China	370	74	58.6
Low-income economies (excluding China and India)	350	72	52.6
Lower-middle-income economies	1,590	46	44.5
Middle-income economies	2,480	38	31.0
Upper-middle-income economies	3,530	27	19.5
High-income economies	21,050	23	4.5
World average:	4,010	49	22.9

Sources: *Statistical Yearbook of China* (SSB, 1994); World Bank (1993); International Labor Office (1993).

moving into the cities. The government also introduced a household registration system (*hukou*) that treated the population separately in urban compared to rural areas, so that the number of subsidized urban residents was limited. Under this system, peasants could not change their occupation or residence. Even though most food subsidies have been eliminated by the mid-1990s, the *hukou* system remains as a barrier to migration to the cities, largely because of the housing subsidy (H. X. Wu 1994). As a result, economic growth did not lead to extensive transformation of the employment structure, as is the case in most developing countries.

Based on the official per capita income figures (shown in Table 7), the percentage of China's labor force in agriculture may not be grossly inconsistent with other low-income economies. However, this population and employment structure is inconsistent with China's income level if, instead, we accept that China's per capita income level is somewhere around $1,100 (Lardy 1994) based on purchasing-power parity. Furthermore, China's 1990 census data show that agriculture still employs over 70 percent of the total employed population, rather than the 58.6 percent estimated by the State Statistical Bureau.

Another feature of China's rural labor force is that, owing to unbalanced regional economic development, agriculture's share of the labor force differs widely across regions (Table 8). While the percentage of the province's work force in agriculture has declined dramatically in the eastern developed regions (to about 48 percent, on average), that in the western underdeveloped areas has remained at a very high level (about 68 percent, on average). This suggests that

Table 8. Farm Labor as a Share of Rural Population by Province

Provinces by region	Per capita GDP (yuan)	Share of population that is rural (%)	Agriculture's share of province's labor (%)
East:			
Beijing	6,805	35.1	11.8
Tianjin	4,696	42.0	18.6
Liaoning	3,254	55.9	32.3
Shanghai	8,652	30.9	9.2
Jiangsu	2,858	77.4	44.3
Zhejiang	2,850	83.5	46.9
Fujian	2,264	81.1	53.9
Hebei	1,843	83.1	57.3
Guangxi	1,318	84.7	70.0
Shandong	2,307	82.7	58.4
Guangdong	3,575	80.6	43.0
East weighted average:	2,865	76.2	48.4
Central:			
Shanxi	1,744	74.0	45.4
Jilin	2,071	57.7	46.9
Heilongjiang	2,433	51.4	38.1
Anhui	1,253	82.2	64.3
Jiangxi	1,439	78.8	57.5
Henan	1,377	84.1	65.0
Hubei	1,827	72.8	56.7
Hunan	1,487	83.2	65.6
Nei Monggol	1,712	63.7	53.5
Central weighted average:	1,619	75.5	57.8
West:			
Sichuan	2,126	65.1	65.1
Guizhou	1,356	84.6	66.7
Yunnan	1,009	83.6	77.6
Xizang	1,334	83.8	77.4
Shaanxi	1,486	83.2	77.3
Gansu	1,458	78.4	61.8
Qinghai	1,314	79.8	61.1
Ningxia	1,821	66.0	60.2
Xinjiang	1,635	70.2	61.0
West weighted average:	1,672	74.4	68.1

Note: The criterion for dividing the provinces into the three groups was obtained from the *Economic Green Report* (Annual Rural Analysis Group, 1995) p. 136. Per capita GDP statistics are 1992 data; the shares of population and labor are 1993 data. The regional averages are weighted by population. *Source*: *Statistical Yearbook of China* (SSB, 1994).

as a region's economy develops the percentage of the work force in agriculture declines, as expected. The various states of development represented by the many provinces imply that the particular scenario for agricultural labor absorption by industry will have different regional characteristics.

China's rural population is experiencing higher growth rates than the urban population. Since the mid-1970s, China's "family planning program" has played an important role in controlling population growth, but the constraints associated with this policy are different for urban versus rural residents. In urban areas, the one-child policy is strictly enforced and there are few incentives to have more children, whereas in rural areas, couples may have a second child as long as the children are spaced four or five years apart. It is also the case that children are more in demand in the rural areas. After the HRS was adopted in rural China, arable land was distributed in accordance with the number of workers in each household. The elderly depend more on their children than they do on the collectives. This has resulted in a higher birth rate in rural areas compared to urban areas. Over the period 1989–93, the growth rate of the population averaged 1.01 percent in cities and 1.41 percent in rural areas.

The State Statistics Bureau (SSB) publishes year-end population data on the size of the labor force and its distribution among sectors. These are published annually in the *Statistical Yearbook of China* and are considered official figures. Similar work-force data collected for the fourth *National Population Census* (conducted on July 1, 1990, and published through the Population Census Office) differ dramatically from the SSB *Yearbook* data.

The census data are likely to be more accurate than the official SSB figures. If this is indeed the case, then the size of the rural labor force (and possibly the extent of the problem of excess labor in agriculture) is likely to be much greater than what can be inferred from the SSB *Yearbook* data. Table 9 provides a comparison of the two sets of data. The comparison provided by Table 9 clearly indicates that the actual size of the rural labor force is likely to be underreported in the SSB *Yearbook*. If we accept the census data, which should be more reliable, the rural labor force is about 100 million more than the generally accepted SSB figure.

This view is supported by some information contained in the SSB *Yearbook* itself. In a chapter entitled "People's Livelihood," the Rural Household Survey data show that the "support ratio" (i.e., the number of persons supported by a worker, including himself or herself) ranges between 1.64 and 1.66 over the 1989–92 time period (see Table 10 for detailed statistics).

The SSB *Yearbook* sample covers 66,478 households across the nation, and the resulting household support ratio is thus quite plausible. When the support ratio of 1.64 is applied to the 1990 rural population figures, the resulting num-

Table 9. Comparison of *National Population Census* and *Statistical Yearbook of China* Data on Rural Labor (millions)

Description	Yearbook data chaps. 1 & 4[a] (year-end 1990)	Yearbook data chap. 11[b] (year-end 1990)	1990 Census data (July 1, 1990)
Total population	1,143.33	n.a.	1,130.51
Rural population	841.42	895.90	834.37[c]
Total employed	567.40	n.a.	647.24
Total rural employed	420.10	420.10	480.85[c]
Total employed in agriculture[d]	341.17	n.a.	458.16
Total rural employed in FFAF[d]	n.a.	333.36	421.45[c]

[a]Chap. 1, "Population" (p. 59), and chap. 4, "Employment and Wage" (pp. 84–86) (SSB, 1994).
[b]Chap. 11, "Agriculture" (pp. 327–328) (SSB, 1994).
[c]The county population is roughly equivalent to the rural population.
[d]Farming (cropping), forestry, animal husbandry, and fisheries (FFAF).
Sources: Statistical Yearbook of China (SSB, 1994); *Fourth National Population Census* (Population Census Office, 1990).

Table 10. Rural Household Support Ratio, 1989–1992

Year	Sample no. of households	No. of persons sampled	Persons per household	Workers per household	Household support ratio[a]
1989	66,906	325,372	4.86	2.94	1.65
1990	66,960	321,429	4.80	2.92	1.64
1991	67,410	317,816	4.71	2.83	1.66
1992	67,490	315,036	4.67	2.83	1.65

[a]Household support ratio is persons per household divided by workers per household.
Source: Statistical Yearbook of China (SSB, 1994, p. 276).

bers for the rural labor force are 513.06 and 546.28 million (using the SSB's Yearbook's chapter 1 and chapter 11 figures), respectively. Our computed totals are 92.96 and 126.18 million more than the figure totals reported in the *Yearbook*, but are quite close to the *National Population Census* figures.

Excess Labor and Out-Migration from Agriculture

As discussed above, owing to the urban-biased development strategy, the corresponding restrictions on out-migration of agricultural labor, and the finite amount of arable land available to agriculture, excess labor in agriculture has become a significant problem in China. Although a large number of agricultural workers have moved out of the agricultural sector, the growth rate of the agricultural labor force is still quite high relative to the limited cultivated land. From 1978 to 1993, land under cultivation decreased by 4.3 percent, while the number of agricultural workers increased by 16.9 percent. Scholars in China have tried different methods to estimate the amount of surplus labor in the agricultural sector, and their results vary somewhat (Taylor 1993). It is not a straightforward calculation given the paucity of reliable statistical data.

For our analysis of the size of the excess labor problem, estimates of rural-labor supply and demand were made for each province. The results are presented in Tables 11 and 12. Table 11 reports estimates of rural labor demand by province, and Table 12 reports the resulting estimated labor excess. The following steps were used in our procedure:

1. The minimum yearly agricultural labor demand (in millions of workers) was calculated, by province, using the total number of working days required to produce given crops. Data used for calculating these "labor requirements" for production were obtained from the *Agricultural Yearbook of China* (*AYC* Editorial Board). To convert labor requirements into a yearly demand for the total number of workers, it was assumed that farm laborers work either 250 or 300 days per year. Columns (1) and (2) of Table 11 report estimates of total labor demand for crops.
2. The minimum amount of labor demanded in each province was adjusted to account for seasonal demand. This seasonal peak demand for labor was estimated by taking the difference in labor demand between the peak period (July 1) and the end of the year (December 31). The demand for labor on July 1 was obtained from the fourth national census which reported labor employed in cropping on July 1. The December 31 demand was estimated with data in the *Statistical Yearbook of China* on labor employed at year-end. The estimated seasonal peak demand for labor for each province appears in column (3) of Table 11.
3. Labor demand in rural noncropping activities (column [4]) was estimated by subtracting the number of state workers from that of the total labor force working in noncropping activities, as reported in the 1990 national census data. Noncropping activities mainly include animal husbandry, fisheries, and

forestry. Nonagricultural demand (column [5]) was estimated by subtracting the number of agricultural laborers from that of the total number of laborers in rural areas. These data were obtained from the *Statistical Yearbook of China*. Labor in nonagricultural rural activities is primarily that used in the TVEs.

4. The next step was to sum the components in order to arrive at total rural labor demand. The components are comprised of: (a) the minimum labor requirements for cropping; (b) additional labor required for crops during the peak season; (c) rural labor requirements for animal husbandry, fisheries, and forestry; and (d) labor demand in the rural nonagricultural sectors. The estimated total labor demand is reported in columns (6) and (7) of Table 11, for 250 and 300 working days per year, respectively.

The gap between the maximum labor supply and total labor demand was computed, and the differences are reported in columns (5)–(8) of Table 12. To compute the maximum rural labor supply, we used the ratios of rural labor to total provincial labor, obtained from results of a 1990 survey of 66,478 households, conducted by the State Statistical Bureau.

Using this approach, the estimate of surplus labor in agriculture ranges from 139 to 170 million. The latter figure is much higher than most other estimates by China's researchers (see Taylor 1993, p. 286). However, an estimated 170 million surplus workers in the rural area is plausible because it corresponds to related estimates of a total "floating population" of 50 to 100 million alone, which is a subset of the surplus.[1] The estimate of the total labor base in Table 12 is also higher than what is commonly believed, and this partially explains why the approach followed here produces a comparatively large number for the surplus amount of labor.

Under the commune system, because of the lack of monitoring and incentives to work, it was common for people to go to work but do nothing. During this pre-reform period, surplus labor existed but the problem was not very conspicuous. After implementation of the HRS, individual incentives were improved, and as a result the effective labor input increased sharply (Y. J. Lin 1992; McMillan, Whalley, and Zhu 1989). Thus the surplus labor problem became more and more obvious following the introduction of the HRS.

A large number of surplus agricultural workers was absorbed by the township and village enterprises throughout the 1980s. As of 1994, 123.45 million former farmers were engaged in township and village enterprises, accounting for 27.9 percent of the total rural labor force. From 1978 to 1993, the average

---

1 The *Wall Street Journal* (December 12, 1995) reported that China's "floating population" totals at least 70 million.

Table 11. Estimated Rural Labor Demand by Province, 1990 (millions). See pp. 60–61 for explanation.

Province	Cropping demand using 300 days (1)	Cropping demand using 250 days (2)	Cropping seasonal demand on July 1 (3)	Noncropping demand (4)	Nonagriculture demand (5)	Total labor demand in rural areas using 250 days (6) = (2) + (3) + (4) + (5)	Total labor demand in rural areas using 300 days (7) = (1) + (3) + (4) + (5)
Beijing	0.42	0.51	0.21	0.08	1.02	1.82	1.74
Tianjin	0.49	0.59	0.49	0.05	0.81	1.95	1.85
Hebei	9.03	10.83	8.29	0.14	5.80	25.06	23.26
Shanxi	3.41	4.09	3.30	0.10	2.63	10.12	9.44
Nei Monggol	3.62	4.35	1.99	0.53	0.61	7.47	6.75
Liaoning	2.90	3.48	4.28	0.25	2.26	10.26	9.68
Jilin	2.83	3.40	1.71	0.12	0.73	5.96	5.40
Heilongjiang	5.80	6.96	3.34	0.43	0.74	11.47	10.31
Shanghai	0.66	0.79	0.03	0.11	1.75	2.68	2.55
Jiangsu	8.70	10.44	6.83	0.54	10.72	28.53	26.79
Zhejiang	4.94	5.93	−0.52	1.23	6.98	13.63	12.64
Anhui	6.97	8.36	7.15	0.31	3.78	19.61	18.22
Fujian	3.33	3.99	1.91	0.49	2.41	8.80	8.13
Jiangxi	7.64	9.17	3.21	0.34	2.42	15.13	13.60
Shandong	10.80	12.96	13.88	0.34	8.40	35.59	33.43
Henan	10.65	12.78	12.91	0.06	6.04	31.78	29.65
Hubei	9.52	11.42	7.22	0.34	3.37	22.35	20.45
Hunan	10.15	12.18	4.35	1.05	3.41	20.99	18.96
Guangdong	8.40	10.08	4.05	1.09	7.90	23.12	21.44
Guangxi	8.82	10.58	2.88	0.21	1.79	15.46	13.70
Sichuan	15.15	18.18	13.63	0.57	6.56	38.95	35.92
Guizhou	4.18	5.01	2.44	0.04	1.17	8.66	7.82
Yunnan	5.95	7.14	2.31	0.21	1.44	11.10	9.91
Xizang	0.14	0.17	0.01	0.24	0.05	0.47	0.44
Shaanxi	4.35	5.22	3.56	0.13	2.02	10.93	10.06
Gansu	3.75	4.50	3.61	0.16	1.38	9.65	8.90
Qinghai	0.41	0.49	0.40	0.26	0.16	1.31	1.23
Ningxia	0.70	0.85	0.40	0.04	0.16	1.44	1.30
Xinjiang	3.17	3.80	1.19	0.43	0.22	5.64	5.01
National	160.90	193.08	115.06	9.89	86.73	404.76	372.58

Table 12. Estimated Rural Labor Surplus by Province, 1990 (millions). See pp. 60–61 for explanation.

Province	Rural population (1)	Maximum labor supply (2)	Rural labor demand 250 days (3)	Rural labor demand 300 days (4)	Estimated labor surplus 250 days (5)=(2)−(3)	Estimated labor surplus 250 days (6)=(5)/(2)100	Estimated labor surplus 300 days (7)=(2)−(4)	Estimated labor surplus 300 days (8)=(7)/(2)100
Beijing	4.39	2.64	1.82	1.74	0.82	31.15(%)	0.91	34.35(%)
Tianjin	3.99	2.40	1.95	1.85	0.46	19.02	0.56	23.11
Hebei	51.97	31.31	25.06	23.26	6.25	19.95	8.05	25.71
Shanxi	22.69	13.67	10.12	9.44	3.55	25.99	4.23	30.97
Nei Monggol	14.37	8.66	7.47	6.75	1.18	13.69	1.91	22.06
Liaoning	23.09	13.91	10.26	9.68	3.65	26.24	4.23	30.41
Jilin	15.31	9.22	5.96	5.40	3.26	35.34	3.83	41.47
Heilongjiang	19.93	12.01	11.47	10.31	0.54	4.47	1.70	14.14
Shanghai	4.67	2.81	2.68	2.55	0.14	4.80	0.27	9.48
Jiangsu	54.11	32.60	28.53	26.79	4.06	12.46	5.80	17.80
Zhejiang	34.36	20.70	13.63	12.64	7.07	34.17	8.06	38.95
Anhui	48.39	29.15	19.61	18.22	9.54	32.73	10.93	37.51
Fujian	24.80	14.94	8.80	8.13	6.14	41.10	6.81	45.55
Jiangxi	31.11	18.74	15.13	13.60	3.61	19.28	5.14	27.43
Shandong	72.02	43.39	35.59	33.43	7.79	17.96	9.95	22.94
Henan	74.58	44.93	31.78	29.65	13.14	29.26	15.27	34.00
Hubei	43.82	26.40	22.35	20.45	4.04	15.32	5.95	22.53
Hunan	52.07	31.37	20.99	18.96	10.38	33.09	12.41	39.56
Guangdong	54.17	32.63	23.12	21.44	9.51	29.14	11.19	34.29
Guangxi	36.57	22.03	15.46	13.70	6.57	29.82	8.33	37.82
Sichuan	91.16	54.92	38.95	35.92	15.97	29.08	19.00	34.59
Guizhou	28.35	17.08	8.66	7.82	8.42	49.31	9.26	54.20
Yunnan	32.28	19.45	11.10	9.91	8.34	42.91	9.53	49.03
Xizang	1.82	1.10	0.47	0.44	0.63	57.44	0.66	60.04
Shaanxi	26.66	16.06	10.93	10.06	5.13	31.93	6.00	37.34
Gansu	19.22	11.58	9.65	8.90	1.93	16.68	2.68	23.17
Qinghai	3.14	1.89	1.31	1.23	0.58	30.68	0.66	34.96
Ningxia	3.39	2.04	1.44	1.30	0.60	29.31	0.74	36.21
Xinjiang	10.79	6.50	5.64	5.01	0.86	13.25	1.49	22.99
National	903.22	544.11	404.76	372.58	139.35	25.61	171.53	31.53

Table 13. Capital Intensity of TVEs, 1984–1993

Year	Number of employees (million)	Original value of fixed assets (bil. yuan)	Nominal capital/labor ratio (1,000 yuan/worker)	Real capital/labor ratio (1,000 yuan/worker)
1984	52.08	57.5	1.10	1.10
1985	69.79	75.04	1.08	0.99
1986	79.37	94.67	1.19	1.03
1987	88.05	122.66	1.39	1.13
1988	95.46	158.43	1.66	1.13
1989	93.67	192.07	2.05	1.19
1990	92.65	220.20	2.38	1.35
1991	96.09	262.63	2.73	1.51
1992	105.81	346.31	3.27	1.71
1993	123.45	516.09	4.18	1.93

Source: Statistical Yearbook of China (SSB, 1993 and 1994).

annual increase in TVE employees was around 13.1 percent. Because labor migration is strictly controlled by the government, the TVEs have been instrumental in absorbing surplus labor from agriculture. In light of the rapid growth rate of the TVEs, one might expect that they will continue to play an important role in absorbing agricultural labor. However, their ability to absorb surplus agricultural labor may be slowing down.

Although there has been considerable labor movement away from agriculture to the TVEs, about 80 percent of the TVE output is in the coastal regions, so the exit of labor from agriculture is thus regionalized. In addition, the TVEs are becoming more and more capital intensive. The capital/labor ratio, in terms of the original value of fixed assets per worker, has increased from 1,104 yuan per worker in 1984 to 4,180 yuan in 1993 (see Table 13). If deflated by the overall retail price index, the capital labor ratio was about 1,930 yuan in 1993, compared to 1,104 in 1984, which represents an increase of 75 percent in nine years. The capital/labor ratio in Table 13 is the average ratio, and its growth implies an even faster increase in the marginal ratio, suggesting an even greater demand for capital investment for every additional worker employed in TVEs. The capital intensity has increased partly due to rising labor costs in the coastal provinces and partly due to the large amount of international investment capital flowing into China. Given that the capital intensity has increased and the migration of rural labor into the TVEs is slowing down, the future growth of TVEs may not absorb the increasing excess rural labor.

Table 14. Employment Elasticities for TVEs, 1979–93

Year	No. of employees (million)	TVE output (billion RMB) real terms	Elasticity of employment[a]
1979	29.09	54.14	0.94
1980	30.00	62.45	0.89
1981	29.70	67.77	0.91
1982	31.13	76.52	0.93
1983	32.35	90.07	0.88
1984	52.08	147.25	0.98
1985	69.79	223.44	0.88
1986	79.57	276.70	0.92
1987	88.05	359.57	0.85
1988	95.45	435.34	0.90
1989	93.67	438.74	0.97
1990	92.65	484.87	0.89
1991	96.09	576.47	0.87
1992	105.81	858.42	0.74
1993	123.45	1,337.60	0.75

[a]The elasticity of employment is the ratio of the TVE growth rate divided by the growth rate of employed workers.
Source: *Statistical Yearbook of China* (SSB, 1994).

The decreasing ability of the TVEs to absorb surplus labor may be evaluated using another criterion. Table 14 reports employment elasticities for TVEs by period, defined as the ratio of the TVE growth rate to the rate of TVE employment growth. Since the mid-1980s, the TVEs have faced increasingly strong competition from state-owned enterprises and other nonstate sectors such as collective enterprises and private joint ventures. Responding to this situation, the TVEs have been improving their technology by employing more capital rather than more labor. The increase in capital intensity of the TVEs has lessened their ability to absorb surplus labor from agriculture. As a result, employment elasticities of TVEs have been decreasing.

In view of the relative decline in peasants' income, some agricultural economists and policymakers argue that China should protect agriculture in order to promote farmers' income (Chen and Deng 1993; Cheng 1993). In this context, the connotation of "agricultural protection" is to distort the domestic terms of trade in favor of agricultural products. It goes without saying that raising the price of farm produce will raise returns to the specific factor of production—namely land. In a land-scarce/labor-surplus economy like that of

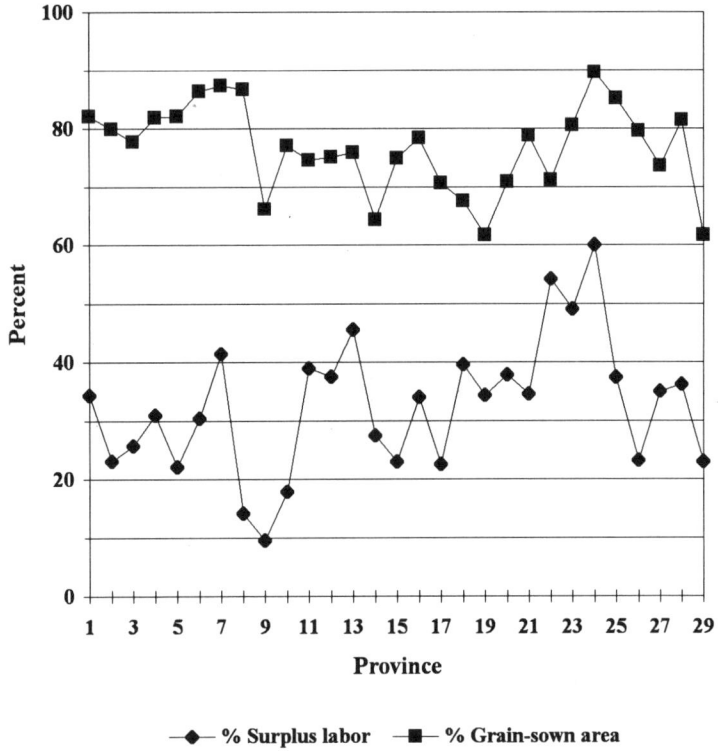

Figure 4. Percentage grain-sown area and surplus labor: by province, 1990. Source: Table 13 and the Statistical Yearbook of China, *1994 (SSB, 1994).*

China, the supply elasticity of labor is very high while that for agricultural land is very very small. Hence, the effect of raising the price of farm products may just result in raising the return to lands and discouraging out-migration of labor (Johnson 1991). In addition, considering the large proportion of the population that is involved in agriculture, it is doubtful whether the government or urban residents could afford to subsidize agriculture.

Policy Options for Addressing the Problem of Excess Labor

From Figure 4 it is quite clear that the magnitude of the rural surplus labor problem is related to the local economic structure—in other words, the larger the grain-sown area, the greater the percentage of surplus labor. Various experiences in other countries with regard to agricultural development show that the patterns of technological innovation and adoption have been diverse across countries with different endowments of essential factors of production. Usually, there are two choices regarding new technologies—either land-saving or labor-saving. The choice depends on the relative abundance and relative prices of factors of production (Hayami and Ruttan 1980; Lin 1991). The current task faced by China's government is to adopt a practical agricultural development policy based on the existence of surplus rural labor.

Generally speaking, with scarce arable land and abundant labor, China has a comparative advantage in certain cash crops produced by using relatively little land and plentiful labor. However, China is so vast that there are different resource endowments among regions, and a comparative advantage in grains may remain in some provinces. China's current agricultural policy of regional self-sufficiency prevents regions from raising incomes through specialization according to comparative advantage.[2] Regardless of whether or not it has a comparative advantage in grain production, each province must continue to maintain its grain supply under China's self-sufficiency policy.

During those years when grain is not in short supply, those provinces with a comparative advantage in grain could transfer surplus grain to other provinces. By virtue of this opportunity, the grain deficit provinces could extend their production of cash crops according to their comparative advantage. During those years when grain is in short supply, this regional labor division would be restrained (Cai 1992; Carter and Zhong 1991b).

In the case of China, grain crops occupy a large amount of arable land, relative to cash crops.[3] Once the government strictly controls the sown area of grains by requiring each province to maintain self-sufficiency, the comparative advantage is lost. The policy choice for overcoming the comparative disadvantage in agriculture and making full use of the labor supply is to abolish the self-sufficiency policy in agriculture and initiate agricultural trade liberalization (Garnaut, Huang, and Cai 1995). This strategy would provide a logical foundation for establishing a policy to solve the problem of labor surplus in the immediate future.

---

2 The policy is reflected in the allocation of grain and cotton production plans and procurement quotas, and the goal of regional self-sufficiency was reiterated at the 1995 session of the People's Congress, where it was announced that provincial governors are responsible for the grain supply in each province.
3 According to the survey on production costs in agriculture conducted in 1991, among grain crops, it cost 12.3 WD (working days) units to produce wheat on one mu (1/15 ha), 18.2 to produce rice, and 13.8 to produce corn; among cash crops, it cost 38.44 working days for the production of cotton, 40.4 for sugar cane, and 235.6 for tea (*Ministry of Agriculture*, 1992).

Summary

The potential for labor mobility is enormous in China. Whether China is considered to be a low-income or a middle-income developing country, its urbanization level is still lower than what it should be in terms of its stage of development. The urbanization level could be expanded by further developing manufacturing and tertiary industries. The share of services in China's GDP is about 30 percent, which ranks with the lowest in the world. This suggests a great potential for China to promote urbanization through expansion of the service sector.

To achieve any measure of success in the promotion of urbanization, the institutional obstacles must be overcome. As discussed earlier, the Chinese government imposed a household registration system to enforce its policy of urban–rural separation. This system has prevented peasants from changing their occupation or their residence, and has produced a dual labor market. Complementing this household registration system, a number of urban-biased policies have been implemented, including: (a) an employment policy that excludes rural residents; (b) a housing subsidy policy; (c) free medicare, and education; (d) subsidies for infrastructure like transportation and utilities; and (e) an exclusive low-price ration system for basic foods. Since the economic reforms, some of these policies have gradually been abolished or have been loosened up. For instance, a market-based housing system has appeared in some regions, and the official distribution channel is no longer the only feasible way to obtain housing in the larger cities of China.

Reforms of these urban-biased policies would encourage rapid urbanization. Because of the obstacles to permanent rural out-migration described above, recent urbanization has been characterized by the expansion of small towns and by increases in the temporary "floating" population in the cities. The central government and city authorities clearly have failed to recognize the contribution made by peasants to urban industry for the past several decades.

CHAPTER 6

Township and Village Enterprises

During the commune era, to enhance the self-sufficient characteristic of the rural people's commune, small-scaled enterprises and shops were established and run by the commune and brigade. Those enterprises were mainly engaged in processing farm products and by-products, and in providing technical services. The Cultural Revolution provided an opportunity for the "commune and brigade enterprises" (CBEs) to expand production and to change their scope of operations.[1] For example, in the southern part of Jiangsu Province, CBEs benefited from chaos in the nearby urban areas, where production of state enterprises was disrupted or even curtailed, and many technicians and skilled workers were sent to the countryside, usually to their original hometowns in nearby regions. Supported by those human resources, CBEs were able to produce consumer goods that were sold in urban markets. However, because those CBEs were heavily regulated by the government, they could not grow as fast as they desired. This changed early in the reform period, when the government lifted restrictions on the now famous TVEs.

China's rural–urban economy is not well integrated, due to distorted prices, imperfect or absent markets, and immobility of factors of production. This is also true of intraregional rural economies, but within an individual region there is a strong linkage between agriculture and the township and village enterprises (TVEs). Since the economic reforms of 1978, the value of industrial output generated by the TVEs[2] has increased rapidly, with an average annual real

---

1 CBEs were renamed TVEs following the collapse of the commune system.
2 According to the *Statistical Yearbook of China* (SSB, 1988, p. 928), the TVEs refer to industrial enterprises where the means of production and the products are owned by workers in TVEs, whereas the state-owned enterprises (SOEs) refer to industrial enterprises where the means of production and the products are owned by all the people. More specific definitions can be found in Rawski (1994). He clarifies that SOEs are enterprises in which the legal ownership of post-tax profits resides in the hands of some level of the government, whereas collective enterprises (mostly TVEs) are those in which this residual ownership right resides with the enterprise itself.

Table 15. Gross Output Value of Total Society, Industry, and Agriculture

Year	Society's output	Industry output	Agriculture output	State-owned	TVEs	Private	Other
	Gross value of			Gross value of total output value of industry			

At current prices, 100 million yuan

Year	Society's output	Industry output	Agriculture output	State-owned	TVEs	Private	Other
1952	1,015	349	461	145	11	71.8	70
1965	2,695	1,402	833	1,263	139		
1970	3,800	2,117	1,021	1,855	262		
1975	5,379	3,207	1,260	2,601	606		
1978	6,846	4,237	1,397	3,289	948		
1980	8,534	5,154	1,923	3,916	1,214	0.8	24
1985	16,582	9,716	3,619	6,302	3,117	179.7	117
1990	38,035	23,924	7,662	13,064	8,523	1,290.3	1,047
1992	55,842	37,066	9,085	17,824	14,101	2,506.8	2,633

Percent

Year	Society's output	Industry output	Agriculture output	State-owned	TVEs	Private	Other
1952	100	34.4	45.4	14.3	1.1	7.1	6.9
1965	100	52.0	30.9	46.9	5.2		
1970	100	55.7	26.9	48.8	6.9		
1975	100	59.6	23.4	48.3	11.3		
1978	100	61.9	20.4	48.0	13.8		
1980	100	60.4	22.5	45.9	14.2	0.0	0.3
1985	100	58.6	21.8	38.0	18.8	1.1	0.7
1990	100	62.9	20.1	34.3	22.4	3.4	2.8
1992	100	66.4	16.3	31.9	25.3	4.5	4.7

Compound annual growth rate in nominal terms (%)

Year	Society's output	Industry output	Agriculture output	State-owned	TVEs
1952–1978	7.6	10.1	4.4	12.8	18.5
1978–1992	16.2	16.8	14.3	7.3	21.3

Compound annual growth rate in real terms (%)

Year	Society's output	Industry output	Agriculture output	State-owned	TVEs
1952–1978	6.9	9.3	3.6	12.0	17.8
1978–1992	10.2	10.8	8.3	6.8	15.3

Note: A blank entry means that data are not available. The real growth rate equals the nominal growth rate deflated by the consumer price index obtained from the *Statistical Yearbook of China* (SSB, 1993, p. 238).

Source: *Statistical Yearbook of China* (SSB, 1993, Tables 9-6, 2-30, and 10-4).

growth rate of 15.3 percent from 1978 to 1992 (see Table 15). The policy changes in agriculture in 1978 provided the basis for the very rapid economic growth of the TVEs, and the TVEs have been the main source of China's dynamism under reform (Chen, Jefferson, and Singh 1992; Findlay, Watson, and Wu 1994; McMillan 1994). The growth rate of TVEs was approximately double that of either urban state-owned enterprises (SOEs) or the agricultural sector.

The government anticipated that growth in TVEs under the favorable policy would result in some profits being diverted toward the subsidization of agriculture, and that the TVEs would be an avenue to absorb excess agricultural labor, and this would boost rural incomes. The rate at which the TVEs create jobs is very critical for the agricultural sector, given the problem of too much labor in agriculture and the restrictions on rural-to-urban migration.

From 1978 to 1993, the total number of TVEs increased from 1.5 to 24.5 million and the number of employees increased from 28.3 to 123.4 million (see Table 16). The TVEs accounted for just 9.2 percent of rural employment in 1978, and by 1985 this figure had more than doubled, indicating that the development of the TVEs has indeed absorbed a large amount of rural labor. On the output side, the TVEs compete with the SOEs, which are mostly located in the urban areas. As a result, the government's policy in the allocation of preferential credit and inputs has always been biased against TVEs and in favor of SOEs.

After the rapid growth in the early 1980s, the increase of TVEs (and their absorption of labor) slowed down in the latter part of the 1980s but then escalated again in the early 1990s. In 1978, the TVEs' share of rural output value was 24.3 percent; this increased to 66 percent by 1992.

The TVEs have helped to maintain agricultural production due to some direct cross-subsidization (e.g., about 10.5 billion yuan in 1992, which is only about 1 percent of the gross value of agricultural output), provision of technical services, and development of infrastructure in the community. However, the TVEs also compete with the agricultural sector for factors of production (e.g., land, labor, fuel, electricity, and capital), and this has had an offsetting negative impact on agricultural output. Usually the TVEs employ the most highly skilled labor in the village, leading to an erosion of the quality of human capital in agriculture. They have also created serious pollution problems for agricultural land and water (Findlay, Watson, Wu 1994, p. 180).

Until now, the TVEs have been viewed as an indirect way to increase farm household incomes. However, efforts to encourage TVEs in the inland and remote areas have often resulted in heavy financial losses. Whereas the gap between rural and urban households is of great importance from a policy perspective, so is the interface between the TVEs and agriculture.

Table 16. TVEs: Major Economic Indicators

Description	Units	1978	1980	1985	1990	1991	1992	1993
Number of TVEs	10,000	152.4	142.5	1,223.0	1,850.0	1,908.0	2,079.0	2,453.0
Number of employees	million	28.27	30.0	69.69	92.65	96.09	105.8	123.45
Share of rural employment	%	9.2	9.4	18.8	22.1	22.3	24.2	n.a.
Gross value of TVE output	bil. yuan	49.31	66.95	275.5	958.1	1,162.0	1,797.5	3,154.1
Share in rural total output	%	24.3	24.0	43.5	57.7	59.2	66.0	n.a.
Profit and taxes:	bil. yuan	11.0	14.4	42.5	101.2	118.8	179.8	178.4
Taxes	bil. yuan	2.2	2.6	13.7	39.2	45.5	63.7	64.9
Profit	bil. yuan	8.8	11.8	28.8	62.0	73.3	116.1	109.3
TVE support to rural communities:	bil. yuan	3.1	4.9	8.3	10.5	12.2	19.0	n.a.
Welfare	bil. yuan	0.4	0.7	2.0	2.4	2.9	4.5	n.a.
Education	bil. yuan	n.a.	n.a.	0.6	1.5	1.8	3.3	n.a.
Subsidies to agriculture	bil. yuan	2.6	2.3	3.0	7.8	8.7	10.5	n.a
Total wages	bil. yuan	8.7	11.9	47.2	113.0	130.5	173.8	132.4

Note: See *Statistical Yearbook of China* (SSB, 1994, p. 362) for the definition of TVEs. It is important to note that figures for 1978–83 include only township- and village-*level* enterprises, as 1984 figures cover *all* township and village enterprises. In the above table, the two rows "TVE support to rural communities" and "Subsidies to agriculture" include only township- and village-*level* enterprises. Therefore, the support to rural communities and subsidies to agriculture are understated.

Source: China's Rural Finance Statistics Yearbook (Agricultural Bank of China, 1992 and 1993).

Total Factor Productivity Growth in TVEs and SOEs

Several studies have been made of the effects of economic reforms on the growth in total factor productivity (TFP) in China's industrial sector.[3] From agriculture's standpoint, it is particularly important to understand the causes for the rapid growth of TVEs, given the strong economic linkage between agriculture and the rural TVEs.

Jefferson, Rawski, and Zheng (1992) compare the growth in TFP between China's SOEs and TVEs over the 1980–88 period. Using industrial gross output and three inputs (labor, capital, and intermediate inputs), they found that the growth in TFP in SOEs was 2.4 percent over that period, which was lower than the rate for TVEs (4.6 percent). Jefferson, Rawski, and Zheng argue that a successful program of economic reforms should generate evidence of gradual convergence in the marginal revenue product of similar inputs across multiple uses. To test this hypothesis, they conducted a comparison of returns to labor, capital, and intermediate inputs across state and collective industries (i.e., TVEs), and found strong movement in the direction of convergency. Hence, they suggest that China's reform may have begun to affect the efficiency of resource allocation despite the limited spread of factor markets.

Woo, Hai, and Jin (1994) use a data set containing production and financial information from 300 large and medium SOEs, and 200 TVEs, in ten provinces over the 1984–88 period. They report that TFP growth in SOEs was at best zero over the 1984–88 period. However, they found a positive growth in TFP for TVEs, between 0.5 percent and 6.4 percent, depending on model specifications. Woo, Hai, and Jin state that the high TFP growth in some studies (e.g., Chen et al. 1988; Svejnar 1990) might be due to incorrect treatment of intermediate inputs. They point out that the result by Chen et al. could have been due to intermediate inputs being overdeflated, and Svejnar's result due to intermediate inputs being excluded from his estimations of gross output production functions. Woo, Hai, and Jin contend that technical efficiency and financial performance are two separate issues. The former could improve while the latter could simultaneously deteriorate. The laborers are working harder, so technical efficiency increases; yet the greater effort is coming about only because the workers are allowed to grab the lion's share of the increased output. Woo, Hai, and Jin report that total labor compensation increased by 17 percent in the

---

3 In the economics literature, "total factor productivity" is often used synonymously with "increased efficiency" or "technical progress." Studies of total factor productivity attempt to measure the contribution of output growth accounted for by growth of inputs such as labor, land, and capital. After the contributions to output growth by measurable inputs are taken into account, the residual output growth is referred to as "total factor productivity."

sampled SOEs over the 1984–88 period, compared with almost zero increase in the TVEs. They assert that this explains why, in a boom year like 1992 (when real GNP increased 12.8 percent), two-thirds of SOEs were running operation losses.

McGuckin and Nguyen (1993) examined post-reform industrial productivity performance in China, using the 1985 industrial census data. They estimated TFP for thirty-nine individual industries consisting of three types of enterprise (state-owned, collective, and private) for the periods 1980–84 and 1984–85. TVEs are included in the category of collective and private enterprises. McGuckin and Nguyen found that annual TFP growth was uniformly greater for collective and private enterprises than for state enterprises (3.87 percent for collective, 2.80 percent for private, and 0.52 percent for state) during 1980–84. However, for the period after 1984, they found that private enterprise continued to grow at a rapid rate, and outperformed both state-owned and collective enterprises in 1984–85. McGuckin and Nguyen also report that both the proportion of technical employees and retained profits have a significant positive effect on productivity growth in China's industrial sector, but that bonuses to labor appear to have a negative effect.

Svejnar (1990) studied the relationship between production efficiency and structure of ownership in TVEs. Using survey data from four selected counties in China, he found no statistically significant differences in production efficiency among the four types of ownership: township and town, village and production team, partnership/family or individual, and joint venture. He also disclosed that group incentive schemes in TVEs, such as fixed wages with a bonus or an internal work-point system, are associated with higher efficiency than individual incentive schemes, such as piece rates or piece rates with fixed wages. This, Svejnar contends, suggests the importance of teamwork for productive efficiency. He also suggests that employment in TVEs has shifted away from the earlier objective of employment generation toward employment levels that reflect the marginal productivity of labor. He claims that TVEs operate with much less featherbedding than SOEs.

Song (1990) compares the differences in economic efficiency between local SOEs and TVEs in the textile industry in Nanhai county in Guangdong. He found much higher profit margins in TVEs than in SOEs. He provides six reasons why TVEs are more efficient than SOEs:

1. TVEs enjoy tax exemptions during the first several years of operation.
2. The welfare system for workers in SOEs offers such benefits as payment of medical expenses, insurance, housing subsidies, and pensions whereas there are none of these in TVEs.
3. Management costs are higher in SOEs due to overstaffing and complicated

managerial structures. By contrast, TVEs spend very little in this area, and often the owner and manager are the same person.
4. SOEs make higher interest payments to banks than do TVEs.
5. TVEs often use low-cost or substandard raw materials.
6. Finally, labor productivity in TVEs may be higher than in SOEs because the comparatively higher wages in TVEs stimulate workers' enthusiasm.

Du (1990) explains the causes of rapid development of TVEs in China. He asserts that the isolated urban and rural economies and separate factor markets gave birth to China's mode of rural industrialization. He identifies three basic elements that enabled the rapid growth of China's TVEs between 1978 and 1985. First is that policy changes permitted key rural factors of production to shift to nonagricultural activities; second, changes in the macroeconomic environment and in market conditions created space for the survival and expansion of TVE industry; and third, and more importantly, structural changes in the TVE itself, combined with the chain effects caused by the initial rise in agricultural incomes, spurred growth.

Islam (1991) investigated regional variations in the development of TVEs in China. He found that infrastructure-related variables (e.g., electricity, roads, and railways) are important factors in explaining regional variations. In addition, he reports that policies aimed at raising productivity in agriculture and provincial locations (coastal provinces) also contribute to the growth of rural industries. However, he contends that the rapid growth of rural industries and the pattern of such growth appear to have unleashed forces contributing to a widening of gaps in personal incomes in rural areas.

Acknowledging that the emergence of TVEs in China increased job opportunities for rural surplus labor and helped to increase rural per capita income, Zhu (1993) points out four problems associated with them. First, she states that in some localities, new TVEs have been created "blindly," that is, they were set up without paying sufficient attention to economic effectiveness, market size, advanced technology, and the availability of energy and raw materials. As a result, these TVEs had to compete with advanced industries in urban areas to gain access to energy and raw materials. Many lost the competition and have gone bankrupt. Second, there has been serious environmental pollution caused by the development of TVEs. Some cultivated land was used for setting up new plants, and some forests were cut down. No sound preventive and positive measures have been taken to resolve these problems. Third, the income gaps between rich peasants and poor ones have widened. Finally, because many highly productive and skilled peasants left farming for TVEs and some land was not used for cultivating crops, agriculture was seriously disrupted and its output decreased, particularly in Southeast China.

Explanations for the Success of TVEs

Chen, Jefferson, and Singh (1992) assert that one of the key lessons to be learned from China's reform experience is that China chose a path of gradual and partial reform, and encouraged the development of TVEs. They point out that the development of TVEs has: (a) mitigated the problem of rural surplus labor and the flight of workers to cities; (b) expanded the scope of market activity, bringing competitive pressure to bear on state-owned enterprises; (c) diffused the potential under the reforms for a growing division between urban and rural areas; and (d) contributed to the economy's export performance. Chen, Jefferson, and Singh argue that China's reform demonstrates that gradual and partial reform can be successful, and that privatizing state enterprises has not been essential for the success of its industrial reform program. They contest the notion that expanding managerial autonomy and incentives and ending the state's monopoly over industry have, to a substantial degree, substituted for the privatization of state enterprises.

Sachs and Woo (1993) argue that it is wrong to suggest that China's reform success demonstrates the merits of "gradualism" as compared with the "shock therapy" undertaken in Eastern Europe and the former Soviet Union (FSU). They claim that it was not gradualism but rather China's economic structure that proved so amenable to reform. China started its reform period as a peasant agricultural society, whereas the FSU started as an urban, (over-) industrialized society. China's two-track liberalization[4] facilitated the flow of peasant agricultural workers to new nonstate sectors, such as labor-intensive and export-oriented TVEs, but the FSU lacked a vast surplus-labor sector. Sachs and Woo contend that the reform in China is a normal economic development; whereas the reform in the FSU is structural adjustment. They argue that in China all major groups can benefit from the flow of workers from low-productivity agriculture to higher-productivity industry.

According to Walder (1994), "conventional wisdom" advocates that the successful transition to a market economy must be rapid and decisive, and publicly owned firms must be privatized if there is to be any hope for economic growth. The only way to reform a socialist economy is therefore through a painful but necessary package of coordinated rapid change, that is, privatization of public firms, credit restrictions, closing firms, reducing employment, and freeing of prices. If the conventional wisdom is right, Walder argues that China has then done all the wrong things: reformed gradually, and implemented cautiously without a coordinated overall plan, which freed prices partially and

---

4 The two-track approach is a strategy that continues state control over the state enterprise sector while permitting the growth of a new nonstate sector largely outside of state control.

which privatized only small proportions of government-owned industrial assets. If China has made such progress by violating this conventional wisdom, how do we account for its success? Walder's answer is "getting the institutions right." In his view, China's experience suggests that, by making government jurisdictions residual claimants, many of the problems of public ownership inherent in a socialist system can be reduced. He further asserts that the experience of China's rural jurisdictions confirms that privatization is not the only way to "get the institutions right." The impressive performance of China's public enterprise system has been achieved for a decade by changing incentives and constraints within corporate hierarchies that include government bodies as owners and often as decision makers. Walder points out that, unlike Eastern Europe and the former Soviet Union, China's decades-long decentralization of industry (even down to the level of the village) provided China, on the eve of the reforms, with a relatively decentralized system of planning and government property rights—with regions and localities already possessing independent industrial bases. Walder argues that this, along with other unique factors such as the high ratio of the agricultural to the industrial labor force and the complete and early dismantling of collective agriculture, makes policy lessons from China difficult to apply to other parts of the world.

The Impact of TVEs on Agricultural Production

Reform brought a change in the government policy toward CBEs and, later, TVEs. The government realized that the procurement prices for farm products might be too low and could not be raised to adequate levels. Consequently it lifted many restrictions on CBEs (and TVEs), hoping that farmers could use the profit to cross-subsidize the farming sector, maintaining the growth trend in agricultural production, especially in grain production. The development was encouraged until the implementation of the rectification program in the late 1980s.

Farmers in subsistence or semisubsistence agriculture, especially when they are facing a compulsory quota, are likely to continue their operation for as long as they are able to survive. In this sense, the income from TVEs may have a positive effect in stimulating (or at least maintaining) agricultural production to some extent. In addition, TVEs may have also contributed to agriculture by providing technical services and improved infrastructure in the community, and by absorbing labor. TVEs typically employ primary workers with the best education in the village, leaving farms to the elderly and women. This differs from the way in which urban enterprises absorb rural workers, as the latter case often leads to migration of the whole family.

Compared with large-scale urban enterprises, TVEs are cost inefficient, as they are scattered over vast amounts of land and require larger investment in transportation and infrastructure facilities, and incur larger costs in shipping inputs and outputs. In the central and western part of the country, the TVEs are usually far distant from major highways or railways. In addition, TVEs occupy larger sites compared to urban enterprises with the same production capacity, and they contribute to serious pollution of the environment, especially to agricultural land and water.

Today, TVEs are still universally viewed in China as the main (or only) way substantially to increase farmers' income. The efforts made in inland and remote areas have often resulted in heavy financial losses. This situation might change if the controls on labor and population migration were relaxed so that the western part of the country could export labor instead of establishing its own TVEs.

If TVEs were to finally concentrate on favorable locations similar to urban enterprises, their negative impact on agriculture would be minimized. However, in addition to government restrictions on migration, the community nature and common-property nature of TVEs in many areas may prevent this from happening, at least in the foreseeable future.

Summary

China's rural–urban economy is not well integrated due to distorted prices, imperfect or absent markets, and immobility of factors of production. This is also true of intraregional rural economies. However, within an individual region, there is a strong linkage between agriculture and the township and village enterprises (TVEs). The TVEs have been the main source of China's dynamism under reform. Their growth rate was approximately double that of either urban state-owned enterprises (SOEs) or the agricultural sector. On the output side, the TVEs compete with the SOEs, which are mostly located in urban areas. As a result, the government's policy in the allocation of preferential credit and inputs has always been biased against TVEs and in favor of SOEs.

After the rapid growth in the early 1980s, the increase of TVEs (and their absorption of labor) slowed down in the latter part of the 1980s but then escalated again in the early 1990s. In 1978, the TVE's share of rural output value was 24.3 percent, and this increased to 66 percent by 1992. From agriculture's standpoint, it is particularly important to understand the causes for the rapid growth of TVEs, given the strong economic linkage between agriculture and the rural TVEs.

CHAPTER 7
Rural Financial Flows

According to McMillan (1994), China's financial system is in a "mess" and the banks' lending patterns often make little economic sense. This observation also applies to the rural financial system. The Agricultural Bank of China was restored in 1979 as part of rural reform; it specializes in rural credit needs, working closely with the Rural Credit Cooperatives, which are located in townships and villages.

Many factors are responsible for the rapid growth of China's agriculture in the early 1980s, and for the subsequent slowdown in the late 1980s. Undoubtedly, the dynamics of capital flows (including income transfers) is a major factor, as they influence farmers' incentives and the capacity and productivity of the agricultural sector. Capital flows out of agriculture take place directly through the banking system and indirectly through income transfers. This chapter will discuss income transfers through pricing, net transfers through the government budget, flows through the financial institutions, and farmers' investment in agriculture.

Income Transfers through Pricing

It is generally agreed that the government procurement of major farm products has been used to extract agricultural surpluses for industrialization. But there are no detailed estimates of the magnitude of such income transfers. Some economists in China have used the concept of the "scissor differential" to describe the difference between the procurement price and the "real value" of farm products, and to estimate the associated income transfers. The scissor differential concept is derived from the Marxist concept of the labor theory of value, which claims that the real value of any product is equal to the socially necessary amount of labor required to produce it. Using the scissor differential concept, Feng and Wei (1993) have estimated nominal income transfers to have increased from 34 billion yuan in 1980 to 78 billion in 1990.

Based on neoclassical economic theory, the difference between the procurement price and the free market is a better approach for calculating the income transfers. The free market for farm products was partly reopened in the late 1970s, but did not function well in terms of price discovery for several years, especially during the first half of the next decade. In addition, some products, such as cotton, still do not trade in free markets. This means there are no available data to estimate the income transfers accurately for all farm products. However, the data for grain markets are relatively good, so we use estimated income transfers through the grain procurement scheme as an indicator of the importance of total transfers.

For grain, it is generally believed that the price difference between the free-market and government procurement price was about 20 to 30 percent in the late 1970s. Relative to the procurement price, the market price trended downward in the mid-1980s, following consecutive bumper harvests. The difference became close to zero, or even negative, by 1984. However, the price difference increased again in the second half of the 1980s. Taking the average of wheat and rice prices as an example, the market price was 10.3 percent higher than the procurement price in 1985, and four years later the price gap had widened to 105.3 percent (see Table 17). In 1990 there was a bumper harvest (which meant that grain production was 10 percent higher than in 1989), and it was also the beginning of a retrenchment program that lowered inflation. As a result, in 1990 the price difference between free-market and procurement prices fell to 66.4 percent.

The data series used for the calculations in Table 17 were obtained from the *Handbook of Rural Economic Information*, and these data ended in 1990. Thus we were unable to estimate the price differences for the early 1990s (and the associated income transfer through procurement). Alternative sources, such as the Statistical Yearbooks, are inadequate because they publish price indexes, and usually the "purchasing" prices are an average of procurement and other purchases. However, in the early 1990s, especially following the 1993–94 inflationary period, the price gap between procurement and free-market prices was believed to have widened again.

In order to obtain a crude estimate of the size of the income transfers, the simple average of rice and wheat prices is used as representative of free-market grain prices. Then, the price difference between the free-market and procurement prices is multiplied by the quota quantity of government grain procure-

Table 17. Procurement and Free Market Prices for Rice and Wheat, 1985–1990 (units: yuan/50 kg)

Year	Procurement			Free market			Average difference[c] %
	Wheat	Rice, in.[a]	Rice, ja.[b]	Wheat	Rice, in.	Rice, ja.	
1985	22.07	15.66	19.90	22.13	20.20	21.24	10.3
1986	21.96	15.70	20.20	26.86	24.22	26.03	33.3
1987	21.96	17.42	21.33	31.04	27.65	30.58	47.0
1988	23.69	17.42	22.28	38.15	36.59	37.05	61.1
1989	25.21	22.45	28.30	53.14	50.50	52.28	105.3
1990	25.21	22.45	28.30	44.51	38.07	43.81	66.4

[a] Indica varieties, unhusked.
[b] Japonica varieties, unhusked.
[c] Calculated as the difference between the average market and procurement quota prices for the three major grains, in percentage terms.
Source: Department of Comprehensive Planning, Ministry of Agriculture, *Nongcun Jingji Ziliao Shouce* (Handbook of rural economic information), 1992, pp. 464–67 and 476.

Table 18. Estimated Rural–Urban Income Transfers through Grain Procurement, 1985–1989

Year	Quantity of procurement[a] (mmt)	Average price[b] (yuan/tonne)	Estimated transfers (bil. yuan)
1985	69.85	384.2	2.76
1986	61.98	385.7	7.96
1987	65.23	404.7	12.41
1988	58.35	422.6	15.07
1989	57.07	506.4	30.43

[a] Quantity procured at the quota price. The data series ended in 1989.
[b] These are the average quota prices (as reported in Table 17 for wheat and indica and japonica rice (unhusked).)
Source: Quantity data were obtained from the Department of Comprehensive Planning, Ministry of Agriculture, Handbook of Rural Economic Information, p. 411. Average quota prices were calculated with the data in the first three price columns in Table 17, and transfers are the product of quantity, quota price, and price difference, which are also listed in Table 17.

ment, in order to calculate total income transfers. The results are displayed in Table 18. Those figures suggest that the government underpaid grain farmers by about 2.76 billion yuan in 1985, through quota procurement alone. Later on, as the price difference widened and the quantity of procured grain increased, the transfers through procurement reached a total of 30.43 billion yuan in 1989, 13.9 percent of the gross value of grain output in that year. Compared with figures from the literature inside China (Feng and Wei; Li 1985; Niu et al.; and Yan), the estimated income transfers in Table 18 show a larger growth in transfers in the late 1980s.

Budget Transfers

Public expenditures on agriculture, especially those on infrastructure, research, and extension, are crucial to the long-term growth in the agricultural sector. The smaller the farm size, the more important the public expenditures will be, as small farmers are more dependent on public investment in quasi-public goods. However, when China's farms were downsized from the average production team size of 17.7 hectares (ha) to the average household size of 0.5 ha during the 1980s, public expenditure on agriculture fell in real terms.

According to the *Statistical Yearbook of China* (SSB, 1993), the nominal budget expenditure on agriculture was 17.4 billion yuan in 1979, and this fell to 11 billion in 1981. Although this figure reached 30.8 billion in 1990, the increase only reflected the high inflation rates during the 1980s. If deflated by the retail price index, the budget expenditure in 1990 was equivalent to 15.1 billion yuan (in 1979 prices), which was 13 percent lower than in 1979. As a result, the share of agriculture in the total government spending declined from 13.7 percent in 1979 to 8.9 percent in 1990. This figure was even lower in 1986 and 1988, at 7.9 percent. On the other hand, the government budget revenues collected from the agricultural sector, including taxes, various levies, and so on, increased from 3.2 billion yuan in 1979 to 12.6 billion in 1990, or by almost three times in eleven years. Combining expenditures and receipts gives the net budget transfers to agriculture. These net figures are reported for the 1979–94 time period in Table 19, where it is shown that significant decreases in net government transfers to agriculture occurred, either in terms of budget share or measured in real terms.

Further data analysis indicates that the nominal budget expenditure on infrastructure facilities declined from 6.2 billion yuan in 1979 to 2.4 billion in 1981, and remained at 3 to 4 billion for the subsequent seven years. Expenditures on infrastructure then reached 6.7 billion in 1990, but the real purchasing power

Table 19. Government Net Budget Transfers to Agriculture, 1979–1994

Year	Expenditure[a] (bil. yuans)	Revenue[b] (bil. yuans)	Net transfers (bil. yuans)	Budget share (%)[c]	Real net transfers[d]
1979	17.43	3.20	14.23	11.4	14.48
1980	14.99	3.31	11.68	9.6	11.02
1981	11.02	3.88	7.14	6.4	6.59
1982	12.05	4.93	7.12	6.2	6.44
1983	13.29	6.76	6.53	5.1	5.82
1984	14.13	6.11	8.02	5.2	6.95
1985	15.36	8.74	6.62	3.6	6.86
1986	18.42	8.04	10.38	4.5	7.80
1987	19.57	9.00	10.57	4.3	7.40
1988	21.41	12.14	9.27	3.4	5.48
1989	26.59	14.16	12.43	4.1	6.23
1990	30.78	12.64	18.15	5.3	8.91
1991	34.76	13.37	21.39	5.6	10.21
1992	37.60	14.95	22.65	5.2	10.26
1993	44.14	23.60	20.54	3.9	8.22
1994	53.30	30.27	23.03	4.0	7.57

[a]From Table 7-10 in the *Statistical Yearbook of China*, 1993, 1994, and 1995 issues.
[b]From Table 7-3 in the *Statistical Yearbook of China*, 1993, 1994, and 1995 issues.
[c]Net transfers divided by total government expenditure data in Table 7-1 in the *Statistical Yearbook of China*, 1993, 1994, and 1995 issues.
[d]Net transfers deflated by the overall retail price index, Table 8-2 in the *Statistical Yearbook of China*, 1995 issue (1979 is used as the base year).

was only about one-half of that compared with the 1979 level. The nominal increase in expenditures on agriculture was basically due to increasing labor costs in supporting institutions, not to increased nominal expenditures related to research and extension work.

The situation becomes even worse if the taxes collected on TVEs are considered as a part of the rural-to-urban transfers. In many cases, collectively run TVEs are providing financial support to the agricultural sector. Therefore, any increase in TVE taxes reduces the net income to farmers and any potential investment in agriculture. When such taxes are included, the total budget transfers to the rural areas were much less than that to the agricultural sector in the early 1980s, and they became negative in 1985 (see Table 20 for detailed statistics).

Table 20. Net Budget Transfers to Rural Areas, 1979–1994 (billion yuan)

Year	Net transfers to agriculture[a]	Taxes on TVEs[b]	Net transfers to rural areas
1979	14.23	2.26	11.97
1980	11.68	2.57	9.11
1981	7.14	3.43	3.71
1982	7.12	4.47	2.65
1983	6.53	5.87	0.64
1984	8.02	7.91	0.11
1985	6.62	10.86	−4.24
1986	10.38	13.73	−3.35
1987	10.57	16.81	−6.24
1988	9.27	23.65	−14.38
1989	12.43	27.25	−14.82
1990	18.15	27.55	−9.40
1991	21.39	33.38	−11.99
1992	22.65	47.02	−24.37
1993	20.54	64.85	−44.31
1994	23.03	107.09	−84.83

[a]Net transfers to agriculture are from Table 19.
[b]Taxes on TVEs are from Table 9-57 of the *Statistical Yearbook of China* 1993; 1993–94 figures are from Table 11-31 of the *Yearbook*, 1994 and 1995 issues.
Source: Calculated by the authors from data contained in the *Statistical Yearbook of China* (SSB, 1993).

Table 20 indicates that the rural economy as a whole received 12 billion yuan from the government budget in 1979, but returned about 15 billion yuan ten years later, in 1989. On a per capita basis, these figures correspond to 10 percent and 3 percent of rural net incomes for the two years, respectively. The situation improved slightly by 1990 but worsened again by 1994.

Induced Capital Outflows

The above analysis suggests that a substantial portion of rural income has been transferred to the public and urban sectors through pricing and budget channels. These implicit taxes reduced the return to investment in agriculture and may have induced even further outward capital flows. Table 21 provides some in-

Table 21. Rural Financial Transfers through Rural Credit Cooperatives, 1979–1993 (billion yuan)

Year	Total rural deposits	Total rural loans	Balance (deposits minus loans)	Annual change in balance
1979	21.59	4.75	16.84	
1980	27.23	8.16	19.07	2.23
1981	31.96	9.64	22.32	3.25
1982	38.99	12.12	26.87	4.55
1983	48.74	16.37	32.37	5.5
1984	62.49	35.45	27.04	−5.33
1985	72.49	40.0	32.49	5.45
1986	96.23	56.85	39.38	6.89
1987	122.52	77.14	45.38	6.0
1988	139.98	90.86	49.12	3.74
1989	166.95	109.49	57.46	8.34
1990	214.49	141.30	73.19	15.73
1991	270.95	180.86	90.09	16.9
1992	347.77	245.39	102.38	12.29
1993	429.73	314.39	115.34	12.96

Source: Total deposit and loans are from Tables 16-8 and 17-9 of the *Statistical Yearbook of China* (SSB, 1993 and 1994 issues, respectively).

dication of the magnitude of financial transfers from the rural to urban areas through the banking system, basically the Rural Credit Cooperatives (RCC). Total rural deposits and loans in Table 21 include deposits and loans from both farmers and TVEs. The transfers in Table 21 do not include those through the Agricultural Bank and hence are incomplete.

From 1980 to 1993, the difference between the amount of deposits and loans increased from 16.8 to 115.3 billion yuan annually (Table 21). In any given year, the year-end balance of rural deposits consistently exceeds the amount of rural loans. This suggests there has been an ongoing transfer of capital from the rural to the urban areas.

The drop in net rural-to-urban transfers in 1984 was due to loans required to purchase large amounts of grain after the bumper harvest. The 1986–89 slowdown in the upward trend of transfers out of agriculture can be explained by the adjustment and retrenchment policy in the TVE sector, which raised the comparative profitability of agriculture for a few years (see Findlay, Watson,

Table 22. Agricultural Financial Transfers through Rural Credit Cooperatives, 1979–1993 (billion yuan)

Year	Farmers' deposits	Farmers' loans	Net farmer deposits	TVE deposits	TVE loans	Net TVE deposits
1979	7.8	1.1	6.7	2.2	1.4	0.8
1980	11.7	1.6	10.1	3.0	3.1	−0.1
1981	17.0	2.5	14.5	3.0	3.6	−0.6
1982	22.8	4.4	18.4	3.4	4.2	−1.0
1983	32.0	7.5	24.5	6.2	6.0	0.2
1984	43.8	18.1	25.7	8.1	13.5	−5.4
1985	56.5	19.4	37.1	7.2	16.4	−9.2
1986	76.6	25.8	50.8	9.2	26.6	−17.4
1987	100.6	34.8	65.8	10.5	35.9	−25.4
1988	114.2	37.2	77.0	12.8	4.56	−32.8
1989	141.2	41.6	99.6	12.6	57.2	−44.6
1990	184.2	51.8	132.4	15.0	76.1	−61.1
1991	231.7	63.1	168.6	19.2	100.7	−81.5
1992	286.7	76.0	210.7	30.2	147.2	−117.0
1993	357.6	88.1	269.5	36.2	200.1	−163.9

Note: Figures represent year-end outstanding deposits and loans.
Source: Deposits and loans are from Tables 16-8 and 17-9 of the *Statistical Yearbook of China* (SSB, 1993 and 1994 issues, respectively).

and Wu 1994, for a discussion of the TVE retrenchment). Afterward, financial transfers out of agriculture speeded up again.

Transfers of capital from agriculture also occurred within the rural economy in the 1980s, as a greater amount of farmers' savings was used by TVEs. By 1993, farmers' total savings with the RCC reached 357.6 billion yuan, but the outstanding total value of farm loans was only 88.1 billion (Table 22). Of the difference, 163.9 billion was used by TVEs, and the rest (105.6 billion) went to other sectors (mainly to the urban areas). Table 22 presents some details on this trend and the data refer to agricultural and TVE transfers, whereas Table 21 reports total rural transfers.

The figures in Table 22 suggest that the annual financial transfer from farmers to TVEs accelerated in the mid-1980s due to the growing gap between the free-market and procurement prices. Returns to farming were falling because of government pricing policy, and resources flowed into other sectors, such as into the TVEs and into urban investments such as stocks and real

Table 23. Individual Farmers' Investments in Agriculture, 1982–1993 (billion yuan)

Year	Total (nominal)	Total (real)	Productive assets (nominal)	Productive assets (real)
1982	19.9	19.9	3.0	3.0
1983	30.5	30.0	6.1	6.0
1984	37.9	36.3	11.3	10.8
1985	47.8	42.1	12.8	11.3
1986	57.5	47.8	7.2	6.0
1987	69.5	53.8	9.2	7.1
1988	86.5	56.5	12.4	8.1
1989	89.2	49.5	9.8	5.4
1990	87.6	47.6	9.9	5.4
1991	104.2	55.0	13.0	6.9
1992	100.5	50.3	6.8	3.4
1993	113.8	50.3	12.2	5.4

Note: The overall retail price index was used as a deflator, with 1982 as the base.
Source: Calculated from data contained in Tables 5-60 and 5-28 in the *Statistical Yearbook of China* (SSB, 1993 and 1994 issues).

estate. These induced financial transfers further dampened the long-run production capacity of the farming sector.

Farmers' Investment in Agriculture

As is the case in most countries, China's government is the major investor in large-scale infrastructure projects designed to improve agricultural production potential. Decisions regarding the construction of small irrigation projects, purchases of farm machinery and equipment, and the like, were shifted from the commune to individual farmers following the reform. The changing pattern in farmers' investment behavior is a good indication of their expectations. Discouraged by the low returns to agriculture, farmers' investment in production capacity declined from the mid-1980s (see Table 23). As can be observed from Table 23, there was a substantial increase in investment in productive assets in the early 1980s, during the early stage of reform, as the situation was generally favorable for agriculture. Investment in productive assets increased in real terms from 1982 to 1985, and also as a share of farmers' total investment. However, the return to agriculture declined afterwards, and thus the investment in production assets also decreased. By 1992, it accounted for less than 7 percent of farmers' total investment, and almost all of this investment was targeted towards housing.[1]

Summary

The most important instrument used by the central government to accomplish income transfers was the relatively low procurement price for major farm products, an approach used from the early 1950s. The total value of such transfers decreased in the early 1980s as procurement prices increased. However, the size of the transfer increased again around 1985, discouraging agricultural production and investment.

Public investment in the agricultural sector, especially in infrastructure, education, research, and extension, is a key factor in agricultural development. However, in China's government expenditures on agriculture declined after the 1978 reforms. There have been significant net financial outflows from the rural areas to the urban areas since 1985. The total annual net transfer in 1990 was roughly equivalent to 20 percent of the GDP generated in the agricultural sector, 35 percent of farmer households' fixed productive assets, and more than ten times farmers' annual investment in productive assets. The income outflows induced further capital outflows through the banking system, because returns to the farming sector have been kept to relatively low levels compared to returns in other sectors, such as TVEs.

Resource outflow from the agricultural sector is a universal phenomenon for developing countries during early stages of growth. However, what happened in China during the late 1980s was unusual in that there was a slowdown in capital outflows but then outflows started increasing again after 1989. The large amount of capital outflows, especially the reduction in public expenditure on infrastructure and extension, has not only contributed to lower growth but also has damaged production capacity.

---

1 See Table 5-60 in the *Statistical Yearbook of China* (1993) for details.

CHAPTER 8
Conclusion

China will continue to be a developing country for a long period of time because its per capita income remains at less than 10 percent of that in high-income countries such as Japan and the United States. It continues to depend heavily on agriculture for economic growth. Food policy is important; over 50 percent of urban residents' income is spent on food, and in the rural area the figure is higher. Although China's economic reform began in the agricultural sector, the recent high growth rates have taken place in the industrial sector. The township and village enterprises (TVEs), located primarily in rural areas in coastal provinces, have been the main source of growth. Further policy reform of agriculture has been unsuccessful since the mid-1980s, and some agricultural reform has been reversed.

China faces some domestic policy challenges in agriculture. The agricultural sector has supported the industrial sector's high rate of growth, and this situation cannot continue without taking its toll on agriculture. Agriculture is a weak sector in China's economy partly because the government still emphasizes both national and regional self-sufficiency in grains. The central government is preoccupied with supplying grain to urban residents, and this bias is manifested in the ongoing conflict between urban and rural residents over grain. As long as the government forces farmers to produce grain, their incomes will be kept low. Relatively low farm incomes and excess rural labor are two of the major problems faced by the government. These are not easy problems to solve. One approach for the government is to deregulate the urban housing market and the *hukou* system, which discourages migration. Alternatively, the government could encourage rapid growth of labor-intensive rural industries. However, there is evidence to suggest that the TVEs are becoming more capital intensive. In any event, large-scale migration of labor out of agriculture is necessary.

The major policy objective of China's market reforms was to speed up economic growth through improved incentives and resource allocation. Industrialization is still at the core of the overall development strategy of the government, and compulsory procurement of major agricultural products is still being used as the major policy instrument to achieve the industrialization goal. The government continues to extract agricultural surplus through the procurement system and relies on political and administrative measures to ensure supply of major farm products. When the low prices result in inadequate supply, the government is forced to increase procurement prices or to implement more rigorous administrative controls. For example, when the grain supply situation became a problem in 1994, the government announced an order prohibiting exports of rice and corn.

Further reform of farm-input markets will result in less government support to farmers. Alternatively, reform of farm-product markets may improve farmers' terms of trade and lead to a relatively larger share of national income being distributed to the farm sector. From the government's point of view, this would slow down the process of industrialization and overall economic growth, and hence contradict its long-run development strategy. In the short run, it might also lead to higher prices in the urban areas and jeopardize social stability. Therefore, any substantial reform in farm-product markets is not likely to occur soon unless there are supply shortages that cannot be corrected without further reform.

In principle, further development of land and labor markets will improve efficiency in land and labor allocation. However, such reform requires significant institutional changes and may lead to instability in the short run, especially in the urban areas. Because social stability is viewed as the precondition for economic growth, any major reform in the land and labor market is not likely to take place in the near future.

Although China has made substantial progress in transforming the economy from a planned to a market-oriented one, especially in the agricultural sector, the government still transfers a large amount of rural income to nonagricultural sectors through the grain and cotton procurement scheme. The direct budgetary transfers also favor the nonfarm economy. In the face of large budgetary pressures, this trend may not be turned around in the near future. The induced financial transfers through the banking system and reduced farm investment in agricultural production are likely to continue. If no major policy changes occur before the end of the decade, the production potential of China's agriculture may be seriously damaged.

References

Agricultural Bank of China. *Zhongguo Nongcun Jinrong Tongji Nianjian* (China's rural finance statistics yearbook). Beijing: Statistical Publishing House, 1992 and 1993 issues.

Agricultural Yearbook of China (AYC), Editorial Board. *Zhongguo Nongye Nianjian* (Agricultural yearbook of China). Beijing: Agriculture Press. Various issues.

Anderson, Kym. *Changing Comparative Advantages in China.* Paris: Organsation for Economic Cooperation and Development (OECD), 1990.

Anderson, Kym, and Yujiro Hayami. *The Political Economy of Agricultural Protection.* London: Allen & Unwin, 1986.

Annual Rural Analysis Group. *Jingji Lupishu: Zhongguo Nongcun Jingji Fazhan Niandu Baogao* (Economic green report: Annual report on economic development of rural China). Bejing: Chinese Social Science Publishing House. March 1994 and March 1995 reports.

Ash, R. F. "Agricultural Policy Under the Impact of Reform." In *Economic Trends in Chinese Agriculture: The Impact of Post-Mao Reform,* Y. Y. Kueh and R. F. Ash, eds., chap. 1. New York: Oxford University Press, 1993.

Aubert, C. "The Agricultural Crisis in China at the End of the 1980s." In *Remaking Peasant China,* J. Delman, C. Ostergaard, and F. Christiansen, eds. Aarhus, Denmark: Aarhus University Press, 1990.

Banister, J., and C. Wu Harbaugh. "Rural Labor Force Trends in China." In *China: Situation and Outlook Series,* pp. 59–68. Technical Report no. RS-92-3, U.S. Department of Agriculture, Washington, D.C., July 1992.

Brown, Lester, et al. *State of the World: 1995.* New York: W. W. Norton and Co., 1995.

Cai, Fang. "Nongye Guimo Jingji De Xianshi Qianli" (Real Potential of Economy of Scale in Chinese Agriculture). *Xiangzheng Jingji Yanjiu* (Township economy study) 4 (1990): 7–11.

———. "Quyu Bijiao Youshi Yu Nongye Chixu Zengzhang De yuanquan (The Regional Comparative Advantage and the Sources of Agricultural Sustainable Growth.)," *Zhongguo Nongcun Jingji* (Chinese Rural Economy) 11 (1992).

Carter, Colin A., and B. Zhang. "Reforms, the Weather, and Productivity Growth in China's Grain Sector." Unpublished MS. Department of Agricultural Economics, University of California, Davis, 1995.

Carter, Colin A., and Funing Zhong. "China's Past and Future Role in the Grain Trade." *Economic Development and Cultural Change* 39 (1991a): 791–814.

―――. "Will Market Prices Enhance Chinese Agriculture?: A Test of Regional Comparative Advantage." *Western Journal of Agricultural Economics* 16, no. 2 (December 1991b): 417–26.

Chen, J., and Y. Deng. "Qiantan Ru Guan Dui Woguo Liangshi Shengchan De Yingxiang He Duice" (On influences of resumption of the GATT membership on grain production and policy response)." *Zhongguo Nongcun Jingji* (Chinese Rural Economy) 9 (1993): 48–51.

Chen, K., G. Jefferson, and I. Singh. "Lessons from China's Economic Reform." *Journal of Comparative Economics* 16 (1992): 201–25.

Chen, K., H. Wang, Y. Zheng, G. Jefferson, and T. Rawski. "Productivity Change in Chinese Industry." *Journal of Comparative Economics* 12, no. 4 (December 1988): 570–91.

Cheng, Guoqing. "Nongye Baohu He Jingji Fazhan" (Agricultural protection and economic development). *Jingji Yanjiu* (Economic research) 4 (1993): 27–34.

Colby, W. H. "Discouraged by IOUs and Pests, Cotton Farmers Cut 1993 Area." In *China: Situation and Outlook Series*, pp. 24–26. Technical Report no. RS-93-4, U.S. Department of Agriculture, Washington, D.C., July 1993.

Crook, F. W. "China's Grain Supply and Use Balance Sheets." In *China: Agriculture and Trade Report, Situation and Outlook Series*, pp. 22–29. Technical Report no. RS-88-4, U.S. Department of Agriculture/Economic Research Service, Washington, D.C., June 1988.

―――. "Could China Starve the World? Comments on Lester Brown's Article." In *Asia and Pacific Rim Agriculture and Trade Notes*. Staff report, U.S. Department of Agriculture, Washington, D.C., September 15, 1994a.

―――. "An Introduction to China's Rural Grain Supply and Use Tables." In *China: Agriculture and Trade Report, Situation and Outlook Series*, pp. 45–51. Technical Report no. WRS-94-4, U.S. Department of Agriculture/Economic Research Service, Washington, D.C., August 1994b.

―――. "Underreporting of China's Cultivated Land Area: Implications for World Agricultural Trade." In *China: Situation and Outlook Series*, pp. 33–39. Technical Report no. RS-93-4, U.S. Department of Agriculture, Washington, D.C., July 1993.

Deng, Yiming. *Zhongguo Nongye Shengyu Laodongli De Liyong He Zhuanyi* (The use and shift of surplus labor forces in Chinese agriculture). Beijing: Rural Literature Press, 1991.

Deng, Yiming (ed.). *Liangshi Liutong: Shichang Jigou De Zhineng He Zhengfu Hongguan Tiaokong* (Grain circulation: Market agent's function and state macro control). Beijing: Economic Management Press, 1993.

Dong, Xiao-Yuan, and Gregory K. Dow. "Monitoring Costs in Chinese Agricultural Teams." *Journal of Political Economy* 101 (1993): 539–53.

Du, H. "Causes of Rapid Rural Industrial Development." In *China's Rural Industry: Structure, Development, and Reform*, W. Byrd and Q. Lin, eds. London: Oxford University Press, 1990.

Economic Intelligence Unit (EIU). *China: Country Forecast, 2nd Quarter 1994*. London: The EIU, 1994.

Fan, S. "Effects of Technological Change and Institutional Reform on Production Growth in Chinese Agriculture." *American Journal of Agricultural Economics* 73 (1991): 266–75.

References

Fei, J. C. H., and G. Ranis. *Development of the Labor Surplus Economy.* Homewood, IL: Irwin, 1964.

Feng, Haifa, and Li Wei. "Woguo Nongye Wei Gongyehua Tigong Zijin Jilei De Shuliang Yanjiu" (A quantitative research on capital accumulation from agriculture for industrialization). *Jingji Yanjiu* (Economic research) 9 (1993).

Findlay, C., A. Watson, and H. X. Wu (eds.). *Rural Enterprises in China.* New York: St. Martin's Press, 1994.

Garnaut, Ross, Yiping Huang, and Fang Cai. "A Turning Point in China's Agricultural Development." In *The Third Revolution of Rural China,* Ross Garnaut and Guonan Ma, eds. New York: Cambridge University Press, 1995.

Guo, S. *Duanque Yu Duice: Zhongguo Liangshi Wenti Yanjiu* (Shortages and responses: Research into China's grain problem). Beijing: People's University Press, 1988.

———. "Dui Woguo Nongye Baohu Xianzhuang De Fengxi (Analysis of Agricultural Protection in China)." *Zhongguo Nongcun Jingji* (Chinese Rural Economy) 3 (1993): 11–14.

———. "Shengtai Nongye De Zhanlue Diwei" (The strategic position of ecological agriculture). Unpublished paper. Ministry of Agriculture, Beijing, China, December 1994.

Hayami, Y., and V. W. Ruttan. *Agricultural Development: An International Perspective.* Baltimore, MD: Johns Hopkins University Press, 1980.

Huang, J., S. Rozelle, and M. Rosegrant. "Supply, Demand, and China's Future Grain Deficit." Paper presented at the fourth IFPRI Workshop on Projections and Policy Implications of Medium- and Long-Term Rice Supply and Demand, Beijing, China, April 1995.

International Labor Office (ILO). *Labor Statistics yearbook.* Geneva: The ILO, 1993.

International Monetary Fund (IMF). "China at the Threshold of a Market Economy." Occasional Paper no. 107, IMF, Washington, D.C., September 1993.

Islam, R. "Growth of Rural Industries in Post-Reform China: Patterns, Determinants, and Consequences." *Development and Change* 22 (1991): 687–724.

Jefferson, G., T. Rawski, and X. Zheng. "Growth, Efficiency, and Convergency in China's State and Collective Industry." *Economic Development and Cultural Change* 40 (1992): 239–66.

Jiangsu Rural Development Research Center. National Rural Reform Experiment, Area Workshop on the Appropriate Land Management Size in Southern Jiangsu: A Case Study (in Chinese). September 1994.

Johnson, D. Gale. "Economic Reforms in the People's Republic of China." *Economic Development and Cultural Change* 79 (1988): S225–S245.

———. "Agriculture in the Liberalization Process." In *Liberalization in the Process of Economic Development,* L. Klause and K. Kihwan, eds., pp. 283–331. Berkeley, CA: University of California Press, 1991.

———. "Does China Have a Grain Problem?" *China Economic Review* 5, no. 1 (1994): 1–14.

Johnston, B. F. "Sectoral Independence, Structural Transformation, and Agricultural Growth: A Comment." In *Subsistence Agriculture and Economic Development,* C. R. Wharton, Jr., ed. Chicago: Aldine Publishing Co., 1970.

Johnston, B. F., and J. Mellor. "The Nature of Agriculture's Contributions to Economic Development." *Food Research Institute Studies* 1, no. 3 (November 1960): 335–56.

Jorgenson, D. W. "The Role of Agriculture in Economic Development: Classical versus Neoclassical Models of Growth." In *Subsistence Agriculture and Economic Development*, C. R. Wharton, Jr., ed., chap. 11. Chicago: Aldine Publishing Co., 1970.

Kawagoe, T., Y. Hayami, and V. W. Ruttan. "The Intercountry Agricultural Production Function and Productivity Differences among Countries." *Journal of Development Economics* 19 (1985): 113–32.

Kueh, Y. Y. and R. F. Ash (eds.). *Economic Trends in Chinese Agriculture: The Impact of Post-Mao Reforms.* New York: Oxford University Press, 1993.

Lardy, N. R. *Agriculture in China's Modern Economic Development.* Cambridge: Cambridge University Press, 1983.

———. "China's Interprovincial Grain Marketing and Import Demand." Staff Report no. AGES-9059, U.S. Department of Agriculture/Economic Research Service, Washington, D.C., September 1990.

———. *China in the World Economy.* Washington, D.C.: Institute for International Economics, 1994.

Lewis, W.A. "Economic Development with Unlimited Supplies of Labour." *Manchester School of Economics and Social Studies* 22 (May 1954): 139–91.

———. "Unlimited Labour: Further Notes." *Manchester School of Economics and Social Studies* 26 (January 1958): 1–32.

Li, Bingkun. "Jiandaocha De Shuliang Fengxi Wenti (Issues on quantitatively analyzing the scissor differentials). In *Nongye Jingjixue Luncong* (Agricultural Economics Forum), issue 6. Beijing: Agricultural Publishing House, 1985.

Lin, Justin Yifu. "Prohibition of Factor Market Exchanges and Technological Choice in Chinese Agriculture." *Journal of Development Studies* 27, no. 4 (July 1991): 1–15.

———. "Rural Reforms and Policy Changes in China's Grain Economy." Paper presented at the third IRRI/IFPRI Workshop on Projections and Policy Implications of Medium- and Long-Term Rice Supply and Demand, Bangkok, Thailand, January 24–26, 1994.

———. "Dynamics of Change and Productivity Effects of Agricultural Liberalization on China's Agriculture." Staff paper. China Center for Economic Research, Peking University, 1995.

Lin, Justin Yifu, Fang Cai, and Zhou Li. "China's Economic Reforms: Pointers for Other Economies in Transition?" Policy Research Working Paper no. 1310, China Center for Economic Research, Peking University, June 1994.

Lin, Y. J. "Rural Reforms and Agricultural Growth in China." *The American Economic Review* 82 (1992): 34–51.

Liu, Jiang (Minister of Agriculture). "Some Problems in Rural Reform and Development." Opening address to the International Conference on China's Rural Reform and Development in the 1990s, Beijing, China, December 3–6, 1993. Printed in *Both Chinese and Foreign Scholars View Rural China*, Miao Jianping, ed., p. 10. Beijing: Huaxia Press, 1994.

McGuckin, R. H., and S. Nguyen. "Post-Reform Industrial Productivity Performance of China: New Evidence from the 1985 Industrial Census Data." *Economic Inquiry* 31 (1993): 323–41.

McMillan, John. "China's Nonconformist Reforms." Policy Paper no. 11, Institute on Global Conflict and Cooperation, University of California, San Diego, December 1994.

McMillan, John, John Whalley, and Lijing Zhu. "The Impact of China's Economic Reforms on Agricultural Productivity Growth." *Journal of Political Economy* 97 (1989): 781–807.

Ministry of Agriculture, Research Center for Rural Economy. "Chinese Rural Reform and Development: Review and Prospects." Paper presented at the International Conference on China's Rural Reform and Development in the 1990s, Beijing, China, December 3–6, 1993.

National Committee for Agricultural Regionalization of China. *Zhongguo Zonghe Nongye Quhua* (A comprehensive agricultural regionalization of China). Beijing: Agricultural Publishing House, 1984.

Niu, Ruofeng, et al. *Zhongguo Jingji Pianxie Xunhuan Yu Nongye Quzhe Fazhan* (Inclined circle of Chinese economy and distorted development in agriculture). Beijing: Chinese People's University Press, 1991.

Oshima, H. "Underemployment in Backward Economies: An Empirical Comment." *Journal of Political Economy* 66, no. 3 (June 1958): 259–63.

Perkins, D. "The Growing Grain Deficit and Its Implications for China's Development Strategy." In *Rural Development in Taiwan and Mainland*, P. Calkins et al., eds., pp. 149–62. Boulder, CO: Westview Press, 1992.

Population Census Office of the State Council and State Statistical Bureau. *1990 Nian Zhongguo Renkou Pucha Ziliao* (Tabulation on the 1990 population census of the People's Republic of China). Beijing: Statistical Publishing House, 1993.

Prosterman, R., T. Hanstad, and L. Ping. "Reforming China's Rural Land System: A Field Report." RDI Report no. 85, Research Development Center, University of Washington, Seattle, November 1994.

Putterman, L. *Continuity and Change in China's Rural Development: Collective and Reform Eras in Perspective.* New York: Oxford University Press, 1993.

Rawski, T. "How Fast Has Chinese Industry Grown?" Working Paper no. 1194, Washington D.C.: The World Bank, 1994.

Rosner, L. P. "Part-Time Farming, Farm Size, and Efficiency in East Asian Agriculture: An Analysis from Taiwanese Farm Record-Keeping Data." Ph.D. diss. Boston University, 1994.

Rozelle, Scott D. "China's Food Policy Reforms and the Changing Balance Between Market and State." Draft paper. Food Research Institute, Stanford University, Stanford, CA, November 15, 1994.

Sachs, J., and W. Woo. "Structural Factors in the Economic Reforms of China, Eastern Europe, and the Former Soviet Union." Paper presented at the meeting of the Economic Policy Panel, Brussels, October 1993.

Schultz, T. W. *Transforming Traditional Agriculture.* New Haven, CT: Yale University Press, 1964.

Sicular, Terry. "Agricultural Planning and Pricing in the Post-Mao Period." *China Quarterly* 116 (1988): 671–703.

———. "China's Agricultural Policy during the Reform Period." In *China's Economic Dilemmas in the 1990s: The Problems of Reform, Modernization, and Interdependence*, pp. 340–64. A publication of the Joint Economic Committee, Congress of the United States. New York: M. E. Sharpe, 1992.

———. "Ten Years of Reform: Progress and Setbacks in Agricultural Planning and Pricing." In *Economic Trends in Chinese Agriculture: The Impact of Post-Mao Re-*

forms, Y. Y. Kueh and R. F. Ash, eds., chap. 2. New York: Oxford University Press, 1993.

———. "Redefining State, Plan and Market: China's Reforms in Agricultural Commerce." *The China Quarterly* (December 1995).

Solow, R. M. "Technical Change and the Aggregate Production Function." *Review of Economics and Statistics* 39, no. 3 (August 1957): 312–20.

Song, L. "Convergence: A Comparison of Township Firms and Local State Enterprises." In *China's Rural Industry: Structure, Development, and Reform*, W. Byrd and Q. Lin, eds. London: Oxford University Press, 1990.

State Statistical Bureau (SSB). *Zhongguo Nongcun Jingji Fen Xian Tongji Ziliao* (Statistical summaries of China's rural economy by counties). Beijing: Statistical Publishing House, 1980, 1985, and 1987–90.

———. *Zhongguo Tongji Nianjian* (Statistical yearbook of China). Beijing: Statistical Publishing House, 1985–95.

Stone, Bruce. "Basic Agricultural Technology under Reform." In Y. Y. Kueh and R. F. Ash, eds., *Economic Trends in Chinese Agriculture: The Impact of Post-Mao Reforms* chap. 9. New York: Oxford University Press, 1993.

Svejnar, J. "Productive Efficiency and Employment." In *China's Rural Industry: Structure, Development, and Reform*, W. Byrd and Q. Lin, eds. London: Oxford University Press, 1990.

Taylor, J. R. "Rural Employment Trends and the Legacy of Surplus Labor, 1978–1989." In *Economic Trends in Chinese Agriculture: The Impact of Post-Mao Reforms*, Y. Y. Kueh and R. F. Ash, eds., chap. 8. New York: Oxford University Press, 1993.

U.S. Department of Agriculture, Economic Research Service (USDA/ERS). *Agricultural Statistics of the People's Republic of China, 1949–90*. Statistical Bulletin no. 844, USDA/ERS, Washington, D.C., 1992.

Walder, A. "The Varieties of Public Enterprises in China: An Institutional Analysis." Working paper. Harvard University, Cambridge, MA, January 1994.

Watson, A. "China's Economic Reforms, 1987–1993: Growth and Cycles." *Asian-Pacific Economic Review* 8, no. 1 (1994): 57–65.

Wen, G. J. "Total Factor Productivity Change in China's Farming Sector: 1952–1989." *Economic Development and Cultural Change* 42 (1993): 1–41.

West, L.A. "Reform of China's Foreign Trade System." CIR Staff Paper no. 69, Center for International Research, U.S. Bureau of the Census, Washington, D.C., October 1993.

Woo, W., W. Hai, and Y. Jin. "How Successful Has Chinese Enterprise Reform Been? Pitfalls in Opposite Biases and Focus." *Journal of Comparative Economics* 18, no. 3 (June 1994): 410–37.

The World Bank. *World Development Report*, 1993. London: Oxford University Press, 1993.

Wu, Harry Xiaoying. "Rural-to-Urban Migration in the People's Republic of China." *China Quarterly* 139 (September 1994): 669–98.

Wu, Shuo. "Inter-provincial Grain Shipments and Wholesale Markets in China." Paper presented at the International Conference on China's Rural Reform and Development in the 1990s, Beijing, China, December 3–6, 1993.

Yan, Ruizhen, et al. "Zhongguo Gong-Nongye Chanping Jiage Jiandaocha De Xianzhuabg, Qushi He Duice" (Current situations and trends in Chinese industrial-agricultural prices' scissor differentials, and countermeasures). *Jingji Yanjiu* (Economic Research) 2 (1990).

Yao, Shujie. *Agricultural Reforms and Grain Production in China.* New York: St. Martin's Press, 1994.

Ye, Q., and S. Rozelle. "Fertilizer Demand in China's Reforming Economy." *Canadian Journal of Agricultural Economics* 42 (1994): 191–207.

Zhu, M. "Non-Agricultural Industrial Development in Chinese Rural Areas." *Development Policy Review* 11 (1993): 383–92.

Index

advance payments, 47–48
Agricultural Bank of China, 47, 79
Agricultural Input Corporations, 48
agricultural sector:
   and policy challenges, 89–90
   since reforms of 1978, 3, 69
   support of industry by, 1, 14, 20, 49–50, 79–80
   See also specific topic
Anderson, Kym, 2, 27
Annual Rural Analysis Group, 54
arable land, 36, 27
Ash, R. F., 9n
Aubert, C., 30

Banister, J., 53
banking reform, 16
Baogan Dao Hu system. *See* household responsibility system
blockade, rice and corn, 19, 27, 50, 90
Brown, Lester, 5
budget transfers, 82–84, 84*t*

Cai, Fang, 1, 37, 67
capital outflows, 6, 84–87, 88
Carter, Colin A., 3, 26, 30, 32, 34, 67
census data, 55, 58–59, 59*t*
Chen, J., 65
Chen, K., 71, 73, 76
Cheng, Guoqing, 65
Colby, W. H., 44
collective farm management, 9
commodities, zero-quota, 3

commodity pricing, 3, 16, 48
communal farming, 8, 23
commune and brigade enterprises (CBEs), 69. *See also* township and village-owned firms
communication facilities, 25
Comprehensive Agricultural Regionalization of China, 32
conservation, 21, 71, 75
contracts:
   state, 17, 36
   volunteer, 31
corn blockade, 19, 27, 50, 90
cotton war, 44
county-level production analysis, 32–34
Crook, F. W., 5, 35n, 49
crop farming, 11
cunmin xiaozu (production team), 10–11

Da Baogan system. *See* household responsibility system
data inconsistencies, 55, 58–59, 59*t*, 80–82
deficit: grain, 5–6
Deng, Yiming, 49, 53, 65
discrimination, employment, 22
Dong, Xiao-Yuan, 31
Dow, Gregory K., 31
Du, H., 75
dual-track commodity pricing, 3, 16, 48

economic reform:
   First Stage (1978–1984), 15–16, 31, 39

economic reform *(continued)*
　overview of, 14–15
　Second Stage (1984–1988), 16–18
　Third Stage (1988–present), 18–20
economic well-being, 3, 7
economies of scale, 24, 36–37
efficiency production, 34, 35, 73–75, 78
enlargement experiment, 37
environmental effects on agriculture, 20–21, 71, 75. *See also* weather conditions
exports, 19, 26–27, 50, 76, 90

family planning, 58
Fan, S., 3, 31
farm household income, 71, 75, 89
farm product categories, 40
farmer(s):
　agricultural investments of individual, 86–88, 87*t*
　and HRS contracts, 10
　and production decision freedom, 12
farms: size of, 21–23, 31, 36, 37
Fei, J.C.H., 54
Feng, Haifa, 80, 82
fertilizer, 30–31, 35
financial co-ops, 10
financial markets, 3, 16, 52
financial performance: efficiency production versus, 73–74
financial system: rural, 79–88
financial transfers, 81*t*, 86*t*
Findlay, C., 71, 85–86
First Stage (1978–1984) economic reform, 15–16, 31, 39
food consumption, 1, 2*t*
food prices:
　between 1993 and 1995, 48–51
　and inflation, 27–28
　urban, 3, 7, 16, 17, 50, 55–56
food production, 7, 89. *See also* production, agricultural
free markets, 41, 42*t*, 45, 49, 50, 80

Garnaut, Ross, 67
government, Chinese:
　infrastructure investment of, 6–7, 20–21, 77, 82–83
　and net budget transfers to agriculture, 83*t*
　and unified procurement commodities, 3, 4, 79–80
governors, provincial: grain production responsibility of, 19, 20, 26, 44
grain:
　deficit, 5–6
　mandatory procurement of, 13, 25, 31, 49, 80
　output of, 5, 24–25, 30, 32, 34, 67
　reserves of, 13, 25, 31, 45, 49, 80
　and sown area and surplus labor, 66–67, 66
　technological advances concerning, 12
　See also grain prices; grain production
grain prices:
　increases between 1993 and 1995 in, 48–51
　and mandatory procurement and reserves, 49, 80
　urban versus rural, 44
grain production, 11, 13*t*
　and First Stage reform, 16
　provincial governors' responsibility for, 19, 20, 26, 44
　and regional advantage, 67
　regional trade balance and, 25–26
Great Leap Forward, 9, 26
gross value of agricultural output (GVAO), 11, 12*t*, 16, 17–18
gross value output of total society, 70*t*
growth:
　in agricultural sector, 1, 6, 11, 30–39, 67
　slowdown in agricultural, 6, 30–39, 67
Guo, S., 21, 30

Hai, W., 73
Hanstad, T., 23n, 38, 53
Harbaugh, C. Wu, 53
Hayami, Yujiro, 27, 36, 67
health insurance, 47
household responsibility system (HRS):
　and agricultural productivity, 31
　characteristics of, 9
　and family size, 58
　and farm fragmentation, 21–22
　and First Stage reform, 16
　and individual farmer contracts, 10
　and infrastructure investment, 20–21
　introduction of, 3
　and land leases, 23

and surplus labor problem, 61
  and tree-cutting incidents, 20
housing, 22, 55–56, 89
HRS. *See* household responsibility system
Huang, J., 5
Huang, Yiping, 67
hukou system (resident registration), 7, 22, 53, 56, 68, 89

imports:
  estimates of grain, 5
  wheat, 26–27
imposed purchases (*pai gou*), 40
incentives, group, 74
income:
  farm household, 71, 75, 89
  transfers of, 79–82
  urban versus rural, 4t, 5, 6, 56t, 81t
industry:
  agricultural sector's support of, 1, 14, 20, 49–50, 79–80
  capital outflows from agriculture to, 6
  government priority to, 55, 89–90
  and gross value output of total society, 70t
  pollution by, 21, 71, 75
  in Second Stage economic reform, 17
inflation, 16, 19, 27–28, 36, 49
infrastructure: government investment in, 6–7, 20–21, 77, 82–83
inputs: farm, 41, 46–48
international trade, 26–28
investment:
  of Chinese government, 6–7, 20–21, 31, 37–38, 77, 82–83
  and HRS, 20–21
  in infrastructure, 6–7, 20–21, 77, 82–83
  international, 64
  in irrigation, 6–7, 20–21
  long-term, 24
  private, 25
  and rectification program, 18
Islam, R., 75

Jefferson, G., 71, 73, 76
Jiangsu Rural Development Research Center, 37
Jin, Y., 73
Johnson, D. Gale, 30
Johnston, B. F., 54
Jorgenson, D. W., 54–55

Kawagoe, T., 36

labor:
  estimated demand and supply by province, 60–61, 62t, 63t
  excess rural, 6, 37, 53, 60–66, 62t, 63t, 66–67, 66t, 71, 75, 76, 77, 89
  as government problem, 89
  and grain sown area and surplus labor, 66–67, 66t
  immobility of, 7, 22
  and migration and property rights, 23–24, 55–56
  and out-migration from agriculture, 60–66
  overview of, 53–55, 68
  policy options for addressing problems about, 66–67
  and public utility facilities, 47
  and rural population, 55–59
  and seasonal employment, 46–47
  transient, 47
  and TVEs, 71, 75, 76, 77
  and work permits, 22–23
labor bonuses, 74
labor theory of value, 80
land fragmentation, 21–22
land leases, 24
land reconsolidation, 22
land supply elasticity, 65–66
land tenure, 23–24, 39
land transferability, 46
Lardy, N. R., 1, 5, 25, 26, 56
Lewis, W. A., 54
Li, Bingkun, 82
Li, Zhou, 1
Lin, Justin Yifu, 1, 10n, 32n
  and agriculture production and 1978 reforms, 3, 34
  and disguised unemployment, 55, 61, 67
  and food prices, 49, 50
  and HRS system, 21, 30, 31
Liu, Jiang, 53
loans, 47–48

McGuckin, R. H., 74
McMillan, John, 3, 31, 34, 35, 61, 71, 79
management system: two-tiered village, 22
marginal land, 20

marginal prices, 17
"market reform" school, 31, 39
marketing:
   cooperatives, 36
   and farmers' organizations, 25, 45
   liberalized, 19
   and monopolistic-monopsonistic system, 9
   and resource allocation process, 9
markets:
   and farm products infrastructure, 7
   financial, 3, 16, 52
   and food price increases, 48–51
   lack of, 6
   overview of, 40–41, 51–52
   reform in input, 46–48
   reform of product, 41–45
mechanization level, 32, 36
Mellor, J., 54
Ministry of Agriculture: total domestic grain demand estimates of, 5

Nguyen, S., 74
Niu, Ruofeng, 82

"one-off privatization" school, 31, 39
open-market sales, 3
Oshima, H., 54
ownership structure, 74

partnerships, land holding, 36
peasant revolts, 36
Perkins, D., 30
Ping, L., 23n, 37, 53
pollution, industrial, 21, 71, 75
population:
   farm labor as share of, 57t
   floating, 61, 68
   growth in, 51
   rural, 2, 53
price ceilings: urban retail, 4, 43, 50–51
price increases, 12, 15, 19, 35, 48–51
price ratio, farm output to input, 15t
price recentralization: and Third Stage reform, 18
price stagnation, 31
private investment: in agriculture, 6–7, 25
procurement:
   by State, 45t
   and fixing quantity while freeing price, 43

   free-market, 9, 25
   mandatory, 13, 25, 31, 79–80
   and mandatory market prices, 49–51, 80–82, 81t, 90
   and monopolistic-monopsonistic system, 9
   and price increase, 15, 35
   unified, 3, 17, 40
procurement commodities: government, 3, 4, 79–80
production: and ownership, 74
production, agricultural:
   between 1985 and 1992, 30–31
   cooperatives, 36
   county-level analysis of, 32–34
   diversification in, 20
   efficiency in, 34, 35, 73–75, 78
   freedom in decision-making about, 12
   planners, 10
   and potential policy changes, 90
   and reforms of 1978, 3, 26
   TVEs' impact on, 77–78
   See also grain production
production analysis, county-level, 32–34
production association, specialized, 22
production capacity, 88
production costs, 36
production, industrial, 74
profits, 7, 74
property rights, 23–24
Prosterman, R., 23n, 38, 53
protectionism, 51, 65
public utility facilities, 22, 47
Putterman, L., 3

quota:
   abolition of, 35–36
   above-, 3, 15, 17, 40
   contracted purchasing, 43, 50
   and delivery first policy, 19
   and price premiums, 3, 15, 17, 40
   and required delivery, 17
   zero-commodities, 3

Ranis, G., 54
rationing, 19, 49–50
Rawski, T., 69n, 73
rectification program, 18
reform:
   Cultural Revolution driven, 8
   of farm products markets, 41–45

and farmer(s) agricultural investments, 87–88
  gradual and partial success of, 76–77
  of input markets, 46–48
  See also economic reform
regional development, 56–58
regional trade: domestic, 24–26, 56–58
registration system, 7, 22, 53, 56, 68, 89
research investment, 6–7, 82
reserves, grain, 13, 25, 45, 49
resident registration (*hukou*), 7, 22, 53, 56, 68, 89
resource allocation, 9, 28–29, 73, 89
retail prices: urban, 40–41, 50, 90
revenue-sharing, 16
rice blockade, 19, 27, 50, 90
Rosegrant, M., 5
Rosner, L. P., 36–37
Rozelle, Scott D., 5, 32n, 41n
rural areas:
  household support ratio in, 59*t*
  income gap between urban and, 4*t*, 5, 6, 56*t*, 81*t*
  population concentration in, 2
  and urban economies, 1, 79–87
  wage gap between urban and, 3
Rural Credit Cooperatives, 47, 79, 85, 85*t*, 86*t*
Ruttan, V. W., 36, 67

Sachs, J., 76
Schultz, T. W., 54
"scissor differential," 79–80
Second Stage economic reform (1984–1988), 16–18
self-sufficiency, 7, 8, 13
service sector: expansion of, 68
Shanghai Grain and Edible Oil Exchange, 43
share-holding cooperative, 24
Sicular, Terry, 9n, 31, 41n
Singh, I., 71, 76
slowdown: in agricultural sector growth, 6, 30–39, 67
socialist market economy, 8, 18
SOEs. *See* state-owned enterprises
Solow, R. M., 34n
Song, L., 74
stability, social, 90
state contracts, 17, 36
State Statistics Bureau, 55, 58–59, 59*t*

state-owned enterprises (SOEs), 71, 73–76
Stone, Bruce, 35
subsidization, 2, 14
"subsidizing agriculture with industry," 14
Supply and Marketing Cooperatives, 48
Svejnar, J., 73, 74

taxes:
  agricultural sector, 4–5, 14, 83
  indirect, 4–5
Taylor, J. R., 53, 54, 60, 61
technicians, 74
technology, 67
Third Stage economic reform (1988–present), 18–20
total factor productivity (TFP), 34, 73–76
township and village-owned firms (TVEs):
  and agricultural production, 77–78
  capital intensity of, 64, 64*t*
  development, 14, 75
  economic indicators, 72*t*
  employment elasticities for, 65–66, 65*t*
  and exports, 76
  and financial flows, 85–86
  industrial pollution, 21, 71, 75
  and infrastructure investment, 77
  overview of, 69–72, 78
  property rights, 24
  and reform since 1978, 3
  social programs, 10
  and SOEs, 73–76, 78
  success of, 76–77
  surplus labor and, 6, 61–64
  total factor productivity (TFP) growth in, 73–76
township (*xiang*) structure, 10
trade:
  international, 26–28
  interprovincial, 25–26, 43, 44, 52
  intraprovincial, 7
transportation congestion, 25
tree-cutting incidents, 20
TVEs. *See* township and village-owned firms
two-track commodity pricing, 3, 16, 48

unemployment: disguised, 54, 55, 61, 67
unemployment insurance, 47
unified procurement, 3, 17, 40

urban areas:
    economic well-being in, 3, 7
    food prices in, 3, 7, 16, 17, 50, 55–56
    housing subsidies in, 55–56, 89
    income gap between rural and, 4t, 5, 6, 56t, 81t
    public utility facilities in, 22
    retail price ceilings in, 4, 43, 50–51
    retail prices in, 40–41, 50, 90
    wage gap between rural and, 3, 17, 39
urban enterprises: and employment priorities, 22
urban industrial sector: government-owned, 2
urbanization level, 68

village structure, 10, 22

wage gap: between urban-rural areas, 3, 17, 39
Walder, A., 76–77
Wang, H., 73
warehouses: commercial, 25
water allocation, 10

Watson, A., 31, 71, 85–86
weather conditions, 31, 32–34, 35, 39
Wei, Li, 80, 82
Wen, G. J., 31
West, L. A., 26n
Whalley, John, 3, 31, 34, 35, 61
wheat imports, 26–27
Woo, W., 73, 76
work permits, 22–23
Wu, Harry Xiaoying, 56, 71, 85–86
Wu, Shuo, 24, 25

Yan, Ruizhen, 82
Yao, Shujie, 30
Ye, Q., 32n
yield: increased, 31

zero-quota commodities, 3
Zhang, B., 30, 32
Zheng, X., 73
Zhengzhou Grain Market, 43
Zhong, Funing, 3, 26, 34, 67
Zhu, Lijing, 3, 31, 34, 35, 61
Zhu, M., 75

About the Publisher

THE 1990 INSTITUTE is a U.S.-based nonprofit research organization dedicated to the study of major economic and social issues relating to China. It was conceived in mid-1989 by a group of volunteers who were deeply concerned about conditions in China and wanted to help the people without getting involved in the politics of either China or the United States.

The Institute's mission is to enhance understanding of the economic and social problems that are impeding China's modernization, and to contribute to the search for their solution—through independent, objective, and policy-oriented research—for the benefit of the people of China, and the peace and prosperity of the world. To further this goal The Institute sponsors in-depth studies and holds conferences to facilitate an ongoing dialogue between research scholars in the United States and those in China.

All research projects of the Institute are guided by four basic principles:

- **Goal orientation**: Emphasis on scholarly excellence and practical value;
- **Quality control:** All work to be rigorously reviewed by experts;
- **Independence**: Political, financial, and intellectual independence from special interests;
- **Objectivity**: An open-minded approach and well-balanced presentation.

The 1990 Institute

Honorary Co-Chairs:

Dr. Donald Kennedy   *President Emeritus, Stanford University*
Dr. T. Y. Lin   *Chairman, Lin Tung-Yen China, Inc.*
Dr. Steven Muller   *President Emeritus, Johns Hopkins University*
Dr. Robert T. Parry   *President, Federal Reserve Bank of San Francisco*
Dr. Robert A. Scalapino   *Professor Emeritus, University of California, Berkeley*
Dr. Harold T. Shapiro   *President, Princeton University*
Senator Adlai E. Stevenson   *Former U.S. Senatur (D. Illinois)*
Dr. Chang-Lin Tien   *Chancellor, University of California, Berkeley*

Board of Directors:

Chairman: C. B. Sung*   *President:* Hang-Sheng Cheng*

James M. Arkoosh	John J. Balles*	Jack Beebe
Barbara Bundy*	James T. Caldwell*	Alexander D. Calhoun
Anthony Y. Chan	Floyd T. Chan*	Henry Chan*
Deidra D. Deamer*	Gifford Fong	Walter Fong
Richard Holton*	Teh-Wei Hu*	C. J. Huang*
S. David Kalish*	Rosalyn C. Koo*	Joseph Kwok
Wei-Tai Kwok	David K. Lam*	Stephen T. Lee*
William M. S. Lee*	Margaret Liu	James G. Luce*
Charles McClain	Thomas Moore	Robert Ohrenschall
Pitman B. Potter*	Anton Qiu*	Patricia P. Qiu
Warren Rothman	Andrew I. Sun	Theresa Tao
Kung-Lee Wang	Albert Wen	Jonathan Wilcox
Eric Wong	Jackson Wong*	Hank C. K. Wuh
Camille Tan Yeh	Matilda Young*	

* Founding Members